AAT WORKBOOK

Intermediate (NVQ Level 3)
Unit 7

Preparing Reports and Returns

ISBN 1 84390 075 0

British Library Cataloguing-in-Publication data

A catalogue record for this book is available from the British Library.

We are grateful to the Association of Accounting Technicians for permission to reproduce past assessment material. The solutions have been prepared by The Financial Training Company.

Published by

The Financial Training Company
22J Wincombe Business Park
Shaftesbury
Dorset
SP7 9QJ

Contents

* See Lecturer's Resource Pack

Preface

This Workbook has been produced specifically for Unit 7 of the AAT's Education and Training Scheme.

It is designed to complement the Unit 7 textbook.

The Workbook has the following features.

♦ A Key Techniques question bank which reinforces the main competencies which students must acquire to succeed at this unit.

♦ Six practice devolved assessments.

♦ Two mock devolved assessments.

♦ The answers to practice assessments 1, 3 and 5 and mock assessment 1 have been withheld from this Workbook following discussions with lecturers. These answers are available in the Lecturers' Resource Pack which is available to colleges who adopt our books.

KEY TECHNIQUES – QUESTIONS

1   *Internal and external reports*

Question 1.1

Management require various types of internal reports which aid them in achieving their objectives. These include:

- Regular reports

- Exception reports

- Analysis

- Forecasts

Give an example of each type of report listed above, relating each one to labour cost and/or employee information.

2   *Collecting and organising information*

Question 2.1

Many business systems make use of standard or pre-printed forms. Outline the principles of good form design.

Question 2.2

You work as an accounting technician for a young, expanding SME. Your managing director often sets you 'ad hoc' projects. He asks you to set up an information base of sources of secondary data, particularly those sources produced by government, including the ONS, Office for National Statistics.

Outline the general and specific digests you would include in your information base.

3   *Writing reports*

Question 3.1

You work as an accounting technician for an SME in the agricultural feeds sector of business.

Your company is a member of a trade association and subscribes to the inter-firm comparison scheme.

You have recently received the following report from the trade association.

Agricultural feeds sector		
Ratio	*Company*	*Industry average*
Return on capital employed	26%	24%
Asset turnover	1.63	1.6
% net profit to sales	16%	15%
Current ratio	1.3 : 1	1.2 : 1
Acid test	0.99 : 1	1.01 : 1

Your managing director is a non-financial manager with a technical background and asks you to prepare a report outlining to him the meaning and purpose of each ratio and stating how the company's profitability and liquidity compares with the industry as a whole.

4 Basic processing of data

Question 4.1

Stainsacre Park is an agricultural museum and working farm.

During the month of July 20X1 the visitors to the centre each day were:

520	525	515	515	520	560	525
530	535	520	525	535	555	
535	540	525	535	545	540	
550	555	530	555	545	525	
560	565	525	560	550	515	

(a)   Calculate the range of the figures and produce a frequency distribution using an interval of 5.

(b)   Using the frequency distribution calculated in part (a), calculate the median and the mean values.

5 Tables, charts and diagrams

Question 5.1

Loftus Fertilisers Ltd manufactures three main products 'LF1', 'LF2' and 'LF3'.

Production in tonnes for the last three years was:

		Year	
	20X1	*20X2*	*20X3*
Products			
'LF1'	250,000	300,000	340,000
'LF2'	100,000	125,000	85,000
'LF3'	50,000	50,000	75,000
	400,000	475,000	500,000

Illustrate this information pictorially using:

◆   a component bar chart, and

◆   a compound bar chart

What are the benefits of using each method?

Question 5.2

What principles need to be followed when constructing a table of data to be included in a report?

6 *Graphs, time series and index numbers*

Question 6.1

Runswick Camp is a military museum situated in the North of England. You work as an accounting technician in the business and undertake a number of 'one off' exercises in addition to your routine accounting tasks. The museum keeps a record of visitor numbers per quarter but little analysis has been done on the figures.

The number of visitors to the museum for the past two years were:

20X1	Q	1	5,750
		2	8,950
		3	14,750
		4	6,250
20X2	Q	1	6,550
		2	9,750
		3	15,550
		4	7,050

(a)   Calculate the centred four-point moving average trend figures.

(b)   Prepare a graph showing the trend line and actual number of visitors per quarter to the museum.

(c)   Comment on the trend in visitor numbers.

Question 6.2

Coastal Coaches run a number of services, one of which is a local community commuter run.

The following information shows revenue per passenger over the past three years, together with details of the retail price index for the periods. The total number of passengers per year has remained fairly constant.

Coastal Coaches

	Years		
	20X1	*20X2*	*20X3*
Revenue per passenger	£0.93	£1.10	£1.32
Retail price index	137.7	143.2	147.3

(a)   Prepare a table to show the revenue per passenger for each of the three years and a comparative figure for each year but at year 20X3 prices.

(b)   Present the original revenue per passenger and adjusted revenue per passenger for the three year period in the form of a clearly labelled compound bar chart. If available, prepare your graph on graph paper.

7 *Performance analysis*

Question 7.1

AAT June 95 (adapted)

National Stores Group

The National Stores Group consists of four national chains of stores:

1 **Brighter Homes** are large department stores selling clothes, furniture and other household products.

2 **Happy Life** sell high quality furniture and other decorative items.

3 **Kidsfair** sells children's and babies' clothes and other baby equipment.

4 **Roberts Stores** sell smart, but affordable, clothes for women.

Results for the group for the financial years 20X1 and 20X2 were as follows:

20X1	*Brighter Homes*	*Happy Life*	*Kidsfair*	*Roberts Stores*
Number of stores	143	38	282	241
Total selling area (000 m²)	390	172	118	49
Turnover (excluding VAT) (£m)	623.4	207.4	237.9	94.3
Net profit (£m)	22.4	(12.7)	7.4	1.6
20X2				
Number of stores	135	37	283	241
Total selling area (000 m²)	385	164	119	50
Turnover (excluding VAT) (£m)	638.4	198.7	235.2	98.4
Net profit (£m)	26.4	(9.2)	(3.7)	0.8

Note: There was a negligible rise in the UK RPI between 20X1 and 20X2.

7.1 Task 1

The table below has been devised to show the following information relating to 20X1 and 20X2 for each of the four chains in the group:

(i) Average store size in 000 m².

(ii) Average turnover per store.

(iii) Turnover per m².

(iv) Net profit/turnover ratio.

(v) Net profit per m².

This table has been completed for all four companies below for 20X1 and for Brighter Homes, Happy Life and Roberts Stores for 20X2.

National Stores Group - Profitability Analysis 20X1

	Brighter Homes	Happy Life	Kidsfair	Roberts Stores
Average size of store (000 m²)	2.73	4.53	0.42	0.20
Turnover per store (£m)	4.36	5.46	0.84	0.39
Turnover per m²	£1,598.4	£1,205.8	£2,016.1	£1,924.4
Net profit/turnover	3.59%	(6.12%)	3.11%	1.70%
Net profit per m²	£57.44	(£73.84)	£62.71	£32.65

National Stores Group - Profitability Analysis 20X2

	Brighter Homes	Happy Life	Kidsfair	Roberts Stores
Average size of store (000 m²)	2.85	4.43		0.21
Turnover per store (£m)	4.73	5.37		0.41
Turnover per m²	£1,658.1	£1,211.5		£1,968
Net profit/turnover	4.14%	(4.63%)		0.81%
Net profit per m²	£68.57	(£56.10)		£16.00

Required

Complete the 20X2 table for Kidsfair.

7.1   Task 2

Calculate for the group as a whole:

(a)   Total turnover figures for 20X1 and 20X2.

(b)   Percentage change in total turnover from 20X1 to 20X2.

(c)   Total net profit figures for 20X1 and 20X2.

(d)   Percentage change in total net profit from 20X1 to 20X2.

(e)   Total net profit/turnover ratios for 20X1 and 20X2.

Present your answer in the form of a table.

7.1   Task 3

The management accountant of the group is concerned about the fall in profitability from 20X1 to 20X2. As a project, which she thinks will be helpful to your AAT studies, she has asked you to carry out some analysis of the data available and prepare a detailed report for her.

Required

Write a detailed report explaining the fall in profitability between 20X1 and 20X2 and identifying possible causes of that fall in profitability.

Question 7.2

AAT Dec 98 (adapted)

You are an accounting technician employed by Paper Products Limited, a manufacturing company which uses recycled paper and wood pulp to produce three products:

♦   Toilet tissue
♦   Paper handkerchiefs
♦   Kitchen roll

The company operates from three sites:

♦   East factory, which has three production departments.
♦   West factory, which has one production department.
♦   Head Office, which contains the selling, accounting and administration departments.

You are employed at Head Office and are currently helping the company's management accountant compare the performance of the different departments and factories in the company.

7.2   Task 1

Complete the following table to analyse the performance of the departments and factories in the company. Show your figures to TWO decimal places.

<table>
<tr><th colspan="6">Paper Products Limited
Performance Report year ended 31 October 20X5</th></tr>
<tr><th></th><th colspan="3">East factory</th><th>West factory</th><th rowspan="2">Total</th></tr>
<tr><th></th><th>Toilet tissue</th><th>Paper handkerchiefs</th><th>Kitchen roll</th><th>Toilet tissue</th></tr>
<tr><th></th><th>£m</th><th>£m</th><th>£m</th><th>£m</th><th>£m</th></tr>
<tr><td>Sales</td><td>1.80</td><td>1.60</td><td>0.70</td><td>3.00</td><td>7.10</td></tr>
<tr><td>Costs:</td><td></td><td></td><td></td><td></td><td></td></tr>
<tr><td>Recycled paper</td><td>0.15</td><td>0.18</td><td>0.08</td><td>0.22</td><td>0.63</td></tr>
<tr><td>Wood pulp</td><td>0.30</td><td>0.40</td><td>0.15</td><td>0.55</td><td>1.40</td></tr>
<tr><td>Labour</td><td>0.52</td><td>0.60</td><td>0.32</td><td>0.80</td><td>2.24</td></tr>
<tr><td>Factory overheads (Note 1)</td><td>0.20</td><td>0.20</td><td>0.20</td><td>0.50</td><td>1.10</td></tr>
<tr><td>Head Office costs (Note 2)</td><td>0.10</td><td>0.10</td><td>0.10</td><td>0.10</td><td>0.40</td></tr>
<tr><td>Total costs</td><td>1.27</td><td>1.48</td><td>0.85</td><td>2.17</td><td></td></tr>
<tr><td>Profit</td><td>0.53</td><td>0.12</td><td>(0.15)</td><td>0.83</td><td></td></tr>
<tr><td></td><td>£</td><td>£</td><td>£</td><td>£</td><td>£</td></tr>
<tr><td>Sales per £ recycled paper</td><td>12.00</td><td>8.89</td><td>8.75</td><td>13.64</td><td></td></tr>
<tr><td>Sales per £ wood pulp</td><td>6.00</td><td>4.00</td><td>4.67</td><td>5.45</td><td></td></tr>
<tr><td>Sales per £ labour</td><td></td><td></td><td></td><td></td><td></td></tr>
<tr><td>Profit/sales (%)</td><td>29.44</td><td>7.50</td><td>(21.43)</td><td>27.67</td><td></td></tr>
</table>

Company Accounting Policy
Notes:

1   *The factory overheads at the East factory are shared equally between the three departments.*
2   *The Head Office costs are shared equally between the four departments at the two factories.*

7.2   Task 2

Prepare a report for the management accountant comparing the performance of the departments and factories within Paper Products Limited for the year ended 31 October 20X5.

Your report should be well presented and address the following issues:

♦   a brief assessment of the overall profitability of Paper Products Limited.

♦   a comment on how useful the data is in assessing the overall profitability of the company.

♦   a comparison of the profitability and efficiency of the manufacturing departments at the East factory: toilet tissue, paper handkerchiefs and kitchen roll.

♦   an assessment of how the relative profitability of the departments and factories is affected by company policy on the treatment of overheads.

The sales, total cost and profit figures for Paper Products Limited over the last five years were as follows.

	20X1	20X2	20X3	20X4	20X5
	£m	£m	£m	£m	£m
Sales	6.00	6.40	6.58	7.40	7.10
Total cost	4.20	4.65	5.05	5.80	5.77
Profit	1.80	1.75	1.53	1.60	1.33
Profit/sales (%)					

7.2   Task 3

Complete the table above by calculating the profit/sales (%) for each year. Your figures should be shown as percentages to one decimal place.

8   *VAT administration and registration*

Question 8.1

You work as an accounting technician for a small firm of accountants. Much of your work centres on small and medium sized sole traders and partnerships. You are often involved with the preparation of VAT returns for small businesses.

When accepting new clients you are often asked what records the Customs and Excise require a registered business to keep.

Prepare a checklist of such detail which you can give to clients in answer to this question.

Question 8.2

The following are commonly used VAT terms:

♦   Supply of goods
♦   Supply of services
♦   Output tax
♦   Input tax
♦   Zero rated item
♦   Exempt item
♦   Standard rated

Define clearly each of the above VAT terms.

9 VAT – invoicing and tax points

Question 9.1

The Customs and Excise do not specify a standard format of invoice for registered businesses. However, there are certain essential elements to be shown on a VAT invoice.

List these, explaining clearly the purpose of each.

Question 9.2

Some businesses, particularly retailers, are permitted to issue a 'less detailed tax invoice'.

List the elements which need to be shown on this type of document.

10 VAT returns

Question 10.1

Ray Staniland is a self-employed joiner. He is registered for VAT with registration number 193 5721 74. You are a self-employed licensed accounting technician and Mr Staniland is one of your clients.

His records for the quarter ended 31 March 20X1 showed the following:

Sales day book

	Gross	Standard rated work	Zero rated work	VAT
	£	£	£	£
January	16,187.50	12,500.00	1,500.00	2,187.50
February	16,592.50	13,100.00	1,200.00	2,292.50
March	16,685.00	14,200.00	–	2,485.00
	49,465.00	39,800.00	2,700.00	6,965.00

Purchases day book

	Gross	Net	VAT
	£	£	£
January	7,608.13	6,475.00	1,133.13
February	8,101.62	6,895.00	1,206.62
March	6,762.13	5,755.00	1,007.13
	22,471.88	19,125.00	3,346.88

He informs you that in September 20X0 he wrote off a bad debt for a customer who owed for work done to the value of £1,250 + VAT at 17½%; and asks if it is possible to have bad debt relief from the Customs and Excise.

Task

Complete the VAT form 100 for the period ready for Ray Staniland's signature and prepare a brief note to him outlining how you have dealt with the bad debt relief.

	Value Added Tax Return **For the period**	For Official Use

HM Customs
and Excise

Fold Here

Registration number	Period

You could be liable to a financial penalty if your completed return and all the VAT payable are not received by the due date.

Due date:

For official use D O R only	

Before you fill in this form read the notes on the back and the VAT leaflet *'Filling in your VAT Return'*. Fill in all boxes clearly in ink, and write 'none' where necessary. Don't put a dash or leave any box blank. If there are no pence write '00' in the pence column. **Do not** enter more than one amount in any box.

For official use			£	P
	VAT due in this period on **sales** and other outputs	**1**		
	VAT due in this period on **acquisitions** from other **EC Member States**	**2**		
	Total VAT due (**the sum of boxes 1 and 2**)	**3**		
	VAT reclaimed in this period on **purchases** and other inputs (including acquisitions from the EC)	**4**		
	Net VAT to be paid to Customs or reclaimed by you (Difference between boxes 3 and 4)	**5**		
	Total value of **sales** and all other outputs excluding any VAT. **Include your box 8 figure.**	**6**		00
	Total value of **purchases** and all other inputs excluding any VAT. **Include your box 9 figure.**	**7**		00
	Total value of all **supplies** of goods and related services, excl any VAT, to other **EC Member States.**	**8**		00
	Total value of all **acquisitions** of goods and related servs, excl any VAT, from other **EC Member States.**	**9**		00
	Retail schemes. If you have used any of the schemes in the period covered by this return, enter the relevant letter(s) in this box.			

If you are enclosing a payment please tick this box.	DECLARATION: You, or someone on your behalf, must sign below. I, ... declare that the (Full name of signatory in BLOCK LETTERS) information given above is true and complete. Signature.. Date .... 20............. **A false declaration can result in prosecution.**

VAT 100 (Full)

PCU (June 1996)

PRACTICE DEVOLVED ASSESSMENT 1
Redcar Foods Ltd

This practice devolved assessment is designed to test your ability to prepare reports and returns. You are allowed **1½ hours** to complete your work.

The assessment covers the following performance criteria.

Element 1   Prepare and present periodic performance reports

Performance criteria

1   Information derived from different units of the organisation is consolidated into the appropriate form.

2   Information derived from different information systems within the organisation is correctly reconciled.

4   Transactions between separate units of the organisation are accounted for in accordance with the organisation's procedures.

5   Ratios and performance indicators are accurately calculated in accordance with the organisation's procedures.

6   Reports are prepared in the appropriate form and presented to management within required timescales.

Range statement

1   Information: costs, revenue.

2   Ratios: gross profit margin; net profit margin; return on capital employed.

3   Performance indicators: productivity; cost per unit; resource utilisation; profitability.

4   Methods of presenting information: written report containing diagrams; table.

Element 2   Prepare reports and returns for outside agencies

Performance criteria

1   Relevant information is identified, collated and presented in accordance with the conventions and definitions used by outside agencies.

2   Calculations of ratios and performance indicators are accurate.

3   Authorisation for the despatch of completed reports and returns is sought from the appropriate person.

4   Reports and returns are presented in accordance with outside agencies' requirements and deadlines.

Range statement

1   Ratios: gross profit margin; net profit margin; return on capital employed.

2   Reports and returns: written report; return on standard form.

DATA AND TASKS

The situation and tasks to be completed are set out on the following pages.

The assessment is divided into four tasks.

The assessment contains a large amount of data which you may need to complete the tasks. You are advised to read the whole of the material before commencing your tasks.

Documents provided

You are provided with proforma schedules and report forms for the tasks and these are included in the answer booklet.

The situation

Business:	Redcar Foods Ltd
Location:	Redcar, Cleveland
Personnel:	Owner manager and director – Frank Smith
	Warehouse manager – John Noble
	Accountant – Susan Woodhouse
	Accounting technician – you

The business is a wholesaler of foodstuffs to the catering trade across the North East of England. Its main customers are restaurants, hotels, boarding houses and pubs. The business has expanded in recent years and you have been employed by the company for almost a year.

The main site is based in Redcar, but the company also has a branch in Whitby, North Yorkshire. Most of the buying is done through Redcar; but the Whitby branch also buys in direct from suppliers.

Tasks to be completed

Today is early November 20X1 and the accounts for the year ended 30 September 20X1 have recently been finalised.

You will find an extract from the accounts for this period for each of the Redcar site and the Whitby site in the data below, immediately following the Tasks.

TASK 1

You are required to consolidate this information (combine the accounts for both sites) so as to produce a profit and loss account for the company as a whole.

Note that transfers between the two sites are not to be treated as sales or purchases and are excluded when preparing this statement.

Use the proforma provided in the answer booklet.

Also calculate the ratios incorporated into the report.

TASK 2

Complete the summary sheet showing the main profitability ratios for each site and in total.

The blank schedule is provided in the answer booklet.

TASK 3

The company subscribes to the Foods Federation Inter-firm Comparison scheme.

You have recently received the standard form which needs to be submitted annually. The form is shown in the answer booklet.

Prepare the form ready for Susan Woodhouse's signature.

TASK 4

Once you have completed the form for Task 3, write a short memo to Susan Woodhouse asking her to sign the form, so that it can be sent to the Foods Federation. Use the memo form provided in the answer booklet.

Data

Extract from the accounts for the year ended 30 September 20X1

Redcar site

	£m	£m
Sales		9.45
Opening stocks	1.21	
Purchases	6.72	
	7.93	
Less closing stock	1.73	
Cost of goods sold		6.20
Gross profit		3.25
Wages and salaries	0.95	
Administration costs	0.61	
Distribution costs	0.65	
Other costs	0.10	
		2.31
Net profit		0.94
Capital employed		£3.10m

Included in the sales figure is an amount of £0.55m transferred at cost to the Whitby site.

Whitby site

	£m	£m
Sales		4.65
Opening stocks	0.64	
Purchases (including from Redcar site)	3.27	
	3.91	
Less closing stock	0.75	
Cost of goods sold		3.16
Gross profit		1.49
Wages and salaries	0.41	
Administration costs	0.32	
Distribution costs	0.33	
Other costs	0.04	
		1.10
Net profit		0.39
Capital employed		£2.4m

The average number of full-time equivalent employees in the company during the year was:

Redcar site	73
Whitby site	35

AAT UNIT 7

PRACTICE DEVOLVED ASSESSMENT 1

ANSWER BOOKLET

TASK 1

Consolidated profit and loss account for the year ended 30 September 20X1

	Redcar £m	Whitby £m	Total £m
Sales			
Cost of sales			
Gross profit			
Gross profit as % of sales	%	%	%
Costs:			
Wages and salaries			
Administration costs			
Distribution costs			
Other costs			
Net profit			
Net profit as % of sales	%	%	%
Capital employed			
Return on capital employed	%	%	%

TASK 2

Redcar Foods Ltd
Summary of profitability ratios - Year ended 30 September 20X1

	Responsibility Centre		
Ratio	Redcar site	Whitby site	Total
Return on capital employed			
Gross profit % of sales			
Net profit % of sales			

TASK 3

FOODS FEDERATION INTER-FIRM COMPARISON SCHEME

Annual return – 30 September 20X1

(Express the figures to nearest £000 and % to two decimal places)

Name of business: ....

Financial year end: ....

	£000	
Turnover	....	
Closing stocks	....	
Cost of sales	....	
Gross profit % of sales	...........................%	

Other operating costs	£000	*% of turnover*
Wages and salaries	....	...........................%
Administration costs	....	...........................%
Distribution costs	....	...........................%
Other costs	....	...........................%
Net profit % of sales	...........................%	
Capital employed (£)	....	
Number of employees (full-time equivalent)	....	
Turnover per employee (£)	....	
Average wages and salaries per employee (£)	....	

TASK 4

MEMO

To:

From:

Date:

Subject:

....

....

....

....

....

....

....

....

....

....

....

....

....

....

....

....

....

....

....

....

....

PRACTICE DEVOLVED ASSESSMENT 2
Brompton Fertilisers and Chemicals Ltd

This practice devolved assessment is designed to test your ability to prepare reports and returns. You are allowed **1½ hours** to complete your work.

The assessment covers the following performance criteria.

Element 1   Prepare and present periodic performance reports

Performance criteria

1   Information derived from different units of the organisation is consolidated into the appropriate form.

2   Information derived from different information systems within the organisation is correctly reconciled.

3   When comparing results over time an appropriate method, which allows for changing price levels, is used.

4   Transactions between separate units of the organisation are accounted for in accordance with the organisation's procedures.

5   Ratios and performance indicators are accurately calculated in accordance with the organisation's procedures.

6   Reports are prepared in the appropriate form and presented to management within required timescales.

Range statement

1   Information: costs; revenue.

2   Ratios: gross profit margin; net profit margin; return on capital employed.

3   Performance indicators: productivity; cost per unit; resource utilisation; profitability.

4   Methods of presenting information: written report containing diagrams; table.

DATA AND TASKS

The situation and tasks are set out on the following pages.

The assessment is divided into five tasks.

The assessment contains a large amount of data which you may need to complete the tasks. You are advised to read the whole of the material before commencing your tasks.

Documents provided

You are provided with proforma schedules and report forms for the tasks and these are included in the answer booklet.

The situation

Business:	Brompton Fertilisers and Chemicals Ltd
Location:	North East of England
Personnel:	Owner manager – Zoe Swinglehurst
	Production manager – William Morley
	Warehouse manager – Sarah Buck
	Accountant – Andrew Hill
	Accounting technician – you

The business produces and distributes fertilisers and industrial and agricultural chemicals. It has a manufacturing unit near Scarborough and a distribution unit based in Middlesborough. Both these sites are considered as responsibility centres, ie profit centres.

The manufacturing unit transfers finished goods to the distribution centre at a transfer price based on full production cost. It also sells some products direct to customers.

The company's year end is 31 December 20X5 and today's date is 20 January 20X6.

Tasks to be completed

TASK 1

Immediately following the tasks below you will find an analysis of the monthly sales for the two divisions for the last two years. The figures are exclusive of VAT.

Using these figures you are to complete the sales report form provided in the answer booklet.

TASK 2

Using the blank graph provided in the answer booklet you are required to plot a graph for 20X5 to show, for the company as a whole:

♦ Monthly total of external sales for each month.

♦ Cumulative total of external sales at the end of each month.

♦ 12 month moving totals for each month.

TASK 3

Refer to the incomplete table provided in the answer booklet which shows a summary of turnover for the company over a five year period.

Complete the report to incorporate the sales figures for the years 20X4 and 20X5.

TASK 4

In the data below you will find details of a price index appropriate to the business sector in which the company operates.

You are required to calculate the indexed value of the annual sales at year 20X1 prices, and complete the schedule laid out in the answer booklet.

TASK 5

In the data below you will find an extract from the accounts of the company for the year ended 31 December 20X5.

In the answer booklet you will find a schedule of profitability ratios. The figures for year 20X4 are already shown on the report.

Calculate the following ratios for 20X5:

♦ Gross profit % of sales.

♦ Net profit % of sales.

♦ Return on capital employed.

Write a memo to Andrew Hill focusing on a brief review of performance for past the two years. Use the blank memo form provided in the answer booklet.

Monthly sales over the last two years

20X4	Manufacturing unit			Distribution unit
	Total	External sales	To distribution	Total
	£000	£000	£000	£000
January	215	39	176	320
February	175	51	124	222
March	148	33	115	194
April	191	56	135	249
May	216	45	171	305
June	173	34	139	220
July	135	21	114	205
August	201	38	163	283
September	219	44	175	315
October	175	27	148	241
November	165	23	142	225
December	240	51	189	329
20X5				
January	245	45	200	343
February	158	51	107	194
March	127	22	105	223
April	258	47	211	288
May	226	51	175	275
June	177	39	138	262
July	131	11	120	225
August	222	44	178	318
September	223	42	181	307
October	184	33	151	277
November	195	24	171	257
December	239	51	188	320

Price index appropriate to the business sector

Year	Index
20X1	100.0
20X2	103.5
20X3	107.4
20X4	110.6
20X5	113.7

Brompton Fertilisers and Chemicals Ltd

Extract from accounts for year ended 31 December 20X5

	£m
Turnover	3.75
Cost of sales	2.06
Gross profit	1.69
Administration costs	0.15
Distribution costs	0.27
Other costs	0.01
	0.43
Net profit	1.26
Capital employed	£4.85m

AAT UNIT 7

PRACTICE DEVOLVED ASSESSMENT 2

ANSWER BOOKLET

TASK 1

Sales report (external sales)

Period ended 31 December 20X5

Quarter	Manufacturing £000	Distribution £000	Total £000
January – March			
April – June			
July – September			
October – December			
	————	————	————
	————	————	————

TASK 2

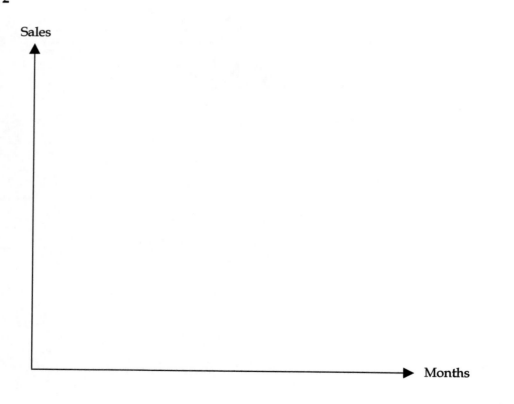

TASK 3

Brompton Fertilisers and Chemicals Ltd

Sales report – five year review

Year	20X1	20X2	20X3	20X4	20X5
Turnover (£000)	3,370	3,410	3,480		

TASK 4

Sales report – five year summary adjusted to 20X1 prices

Year	20X1	20X2	20X3	20X4	20X5
Actual turnover (£000)					
Index					
Adjusted turnover (£000)					

TASK 5

Brompton Fertilisers and Chemicals Ltd

Profitability ratios for 20X4 and 20X5

Year	20X4	20X5
Ratio:		
Gross profit % of sales	44.15%	
Net profit % of sales	32.00%	
Return on capital employed	24.50%	

TASK 5 (continued)

MEMO

To:

From:

Date:

Subject:

....

....

....

....

....

....

....

....

....

....

....

....

....

....

....

....

....

....

....

....

....

PRACTICE DEVOLVED ASSESSMENT 3

Dunsley Pubs and Restaurants Ltd

This practice devolved assessment is designed to test your ability to prepare reports and returns. You are allowed **1½ hours** to complete your work.

The assessment covers the following performance criteria:

Element 1   Prepare and present periodic performance reports

Performance criteria

1   Information derived from different units of the organisation is consolidated into the appropriate form.

2   Information derived from different information systems within the organisation is correctly reconciled.

3   When comparing results over time, an appropriate method which allows for changing price levels is used.

4   Transactions between separate units of the organisation are accounted for in accordance with the organisation's procedures.

5   Ratios and performance indicators are accurately calculated in accordance with the organisation's procedures.

6   Reports are prepared in the appropriate form and presented to management within required timescales.

Range statement

1   Information: costs; revenue.

2   Ratios: gross profit margin; net profit margin; return on capital employed.

3   Performance indicators: productivity; cost per unit; resource utilisation; profitability.

4   Methods of presenting information: written report containing diagrams; table.

Element 2   Prepare reports and returns for outside agencies

Performance criteria

1   Relevant information is identified, collated and presented in accordance with the conventions and definitions used by outside agencies.

2   Calculations of ratios and performance indicators are accurate.

3   Authorisation for the despatch of completed reports and returns is sought from the appropriate person.

4   Reports and returns are presented in accordance with outside agencies' requirements and deadlines.

Range statement

1   Ratios: gross profit margin; net profit margin; return on capital employed.

2   Reports and returns: written report; return on standard form.

DATA AND TASKS

The situation and tasks to be completed are set out on the following pages.

The assessment is divided into five tasks.

The assessment contains a large amount of data which you may need to complete the tasks. You are advised to read the whole of the material before commencing your tasks.

Documents provided

You are provided with proforma schedules and report forms for each task and these are included in the answer booklet.

The situation

Business:	Dunsley Pubs and Restaurants Ltd
Location:	North East England
Personnel:	Owner manager – Pauline Dunn
	Development manager – Philip Rose
	Accountant – Claire Daly
	Accounting technician – you

The business owns a group of 12 pubs, all with restaurant facilities attached. The business sites are all located in and around the North East Coast, ranging from York inland up to Whitby and Scarborough.

The business has expanded in recent years and you have been employed by the company for the past two years.

Tasks to be completed

Today is early February 20X6 and the accounts for the year ended 31 December 20X5 have recently been finalised.

You will find an extract from these accounts immediately following the Tasks below.

TASK 1

In the data below you will find an analysis of company turnover for each quarter for years ended 31 December 20X4 and 20X5.

You are required to calculate the four-point moving average trend figures for the period, and construct a graph showing the trend line and actual turnover, by quarter, for presentation to the accountant.

Use the proforma schedule provided in the answer booklet.

TASK 2

In the data below is a five year summary of company turnover, together with a price index appropriate to the business sector in which Dunsley operates.

Using the schedule provided in the answer booklet, restate each year's turnover in terms of 20X1 prices and calculate the year on year annual increase in sales based on actual and adjusted turnover.

TASK 3

Set out in the answer booklet is a schedule of profitability ratios for the year ended 31 December 20X5.

You are required to calculate these ratios using the accounts shown in the data below and complete the schedule.

TASK 4

The company is a member of a trade association and subscribes to its inter-firm comparison scheme.

In the answer booklet you will find an annual return for the scheme. You are required to complete this ready for Claire Daly's signature and submission to the trade association.

TASK 5

On completing the above return in Task 4, draft a short memo to Claire Daly requesting her signature and commenting briefly on the ratios calculated.

Extract from accounts for year ended 31 December 20X5

Dunsley Pubs and Restaurants Ltd

	£m	£m
Turnover		3.10
Cost of sales		1.36
Gross profit		1.74
Wages and salaries	0.81	
Other operating costs	0.25	
		1.06
Net profit		0.68
Capital employed		£2.90m
Number of full-time equivalent employees		72

Dunsley Pubs and Restaurants Ltd

Analysis of sales per quarter – years 20X4 and 20X5

Year		Turnover £m
20X4	Q1	0.40
	Q2	0.44
	Q3	1.02
	Q4	0.89
		————
		2.75
		————
20X5	Q1	0.45
	Q2	0.49
	Q3	1.15
	Q4	1.01
		————
		3.10
		————

Five year summary of turnover

Year	Turnover £m	Index
20X1	2.10	100.0
20X2	2.25	103.1
20X3	2.51	106.2
20X4	2.75	110.2
20X5	3.10	113.1

AAT UNIT 7

PRACTICE DEVOLVED ASSESSMENT 3

ANSWER BOOKLET

TASK 1

Centred four-point moving average trend figures

Year	Quarter	Turnover £m	Moving annual total £m	Moving average £m	Centred average trend £m
20X4	1				
	2				
	3				
	4				
20X5	1				
	2				
	3				
	4				

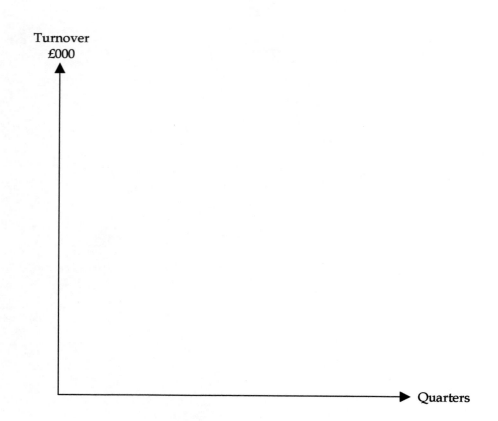

TASK 2

Dunsley Pubs and Restaurants Ltd

Year	20X1 £m	20X2 £m	20X3 £m	20X4 £m	20X5 £m
Actual turnover					
% increase year on year					
Index					
Adjusted turnover					
% increase year on year					

TASK 3

Dunsley Pubs and Restaurants Ltd

Profitability ratios for 20X5

Ratio

Return on capital employed ....%

Gross profit as a % of turnover ....%

Net profit as a % of turnover ....%

TASK 4

TRADE ASSOCIATION INTER-FIRM COMPARISON SCHEME
Annual return – 31 December 20X5

Business name: ....

Year end: ....

(Note: figures are to be shown to nearest £000 and % to two decimal places.)

	£000
Turnover	
Cost of sales	
Gross profit as a % of sales	%

	£000
Wages and salaries	
Other operating costs	
Net profit as a % of sales	%
Number of full-time equivalent employees	
Turnover per employee – full-time equivalent (£000)	£
Wages and salaries per employee (£000)	£

Signature: .... Date: ....

TASK 5

MEMO

To:

From:

Date:

Subject:

....

....

....

....

....

....

....

....

....

....

....

....

....

....

....

....

....

....

....

....

....

....

PRACTICE DEVOLVED ASSESSMENT 4

London Sports Supplies Ltd

This practice devolved assessment is designed to test your competence in preparing reports and returns.

You will be allowed **1½ hours** to complete your work.

The practice devolved assessment covers the following performance criteria.

Element 1   Prepare and present periodic performance reports

Performance criteria

1   Information derived from different units of the organisation is consolidated into the appropriate form.

2   Information derived from different information systems within the organisation is correctly reconciled.

3   When comparing results over time, an appropriate method which allows for changing price levels is used.

4   Transactions between separate units of the organisation are accounted for in accordance with the organisation's procedures.

5   Ratios and performance indicators are accurately calculated in accordance with the organisation's procedures.

6   Reports are prepared in the appropriate form and presented to management within required timescales.

Range statement

1   Information: costs; revenue.

2   Ratios: gross profit margin; net profit margin; return on capital employed.

3   Performance indicators: productivity; cost per unit; resource utilisation; profitability.

4   Methods of presenting information: written report containing diagrams; table.

Element 2   Prepare reports and returns for outside agencies

Performance criteria

1   Relevant information is identified, collated and presented in accordance with the conventions and definitions used by outside agencies.

2   Calculations of ratios and performance indicators are accurate.

3   Authorisation for the despatch of completed reports and returns is sought from the appropriate person.

4   Reports and returns are presented in accordance with outside agencies' requirements and deadlines.

Range statement

1   Ratios: gross profit margin; net profit margin; return on capital employed.

2   Reports and returns: written report; return on standard form.

DATA AND TASKS

The situation and tasks are set out on the following pages.

The assessment is divided into five tasks.

The assessment contains a large amount of information which you will need to complete your work. You are advised to read through all of the situation before commencing your work on this assessment.

Documents provided

A series of blank proformas and schedules are provided in the answer booklet to assist you with the presentation of your answers.

The situation

Business:	London Sports Supplies Ltd
Location:	North Nottinghamshire (head office)
Personnel:	Owner and managing director – William London
	Production manager – Louise Gordon
	Marketing and distribution manager – Amanda Parker
	Accountant – Michael Bateman
	Accounting technician – you

The company produces and wholesales sportswear. The business has three main investment centres, the manager of each being not only responsible for profits but also return on capital.

The site in North Nottinghamshire not only produces some sports clothing but also buys in ready made articles. It sells direct to customers but also deals on an inter-company basis with the other two business units who wholesale sports supplies and clothing. All inter-company transfers are at cost.

The two wholesale centres are based in Sheffield and Birmingham.

You are employed as an accounting technician at the North Nottinghamshire site where all the accounting functions for the company are performed.

Your work is focused on the management accounting needs of the business and you deal with both internal and external reporting. The company's year end is 31 December and it is now late January 20X6.

Tasks to be completed

TASK 1

Immediately following the tasks below, you will find summary operating statements for each business unit for the year ended 31 December 20X5; together with a previous four year review of performance for the group.

Using the schedule provided in the answer booklet, you are required to prepare the summary operating statement for the company as a whole, for the year ended 31 December 20X5. (NB: You need to eliminate the inter-company transfers from your figures.)

TASK 2

Examine the four year review of performance in the data below and together with your results for the year ended 31 December 20X4, prepare a component bar chart in the answer booklet to show an analysis of turnover for the five year period 20X1 – 20X5. (Show the elements of cost of sales, other costs and net profit.)

TASK 3

In the data below you will find a reference to a price index which is appropriate to the sector of business in which London Sports Supplies operate.

In the answer booklet you will find a summary of turnover for the five year period. Complete this table to show turnover for each year but in terms of 20X1 prices.

TASK 4

Refer to the summary operating statements for the previous four years, together with the one you have recently prepared, and prepare the following ratios for the company as a whole:

♦ Return on capital employed

♦ Gross profit % of sales

♦ Net profit % of sales

♦ Administration costs % of sales

♦ Distribution costs % of sales

♦ Turnover per employee

♦ Investment per employee

♦ Net profit per employee

and complete the schedule provided in the answer booklet.

TASK 5

In the data below you will find a memo from Michael Bateman; identify the form to which he makes reference (which you will find included in the answer booklet).

Having read the memo, complete the form in readiness for Michael's signature and send him a short memo informing him of your action. Use the blank memo layout provided in the answer booklet.

Data

LONDON SPORTS SUPPLIES LTD

Summary operating statements for year ended 31 December 20X5

	North Notts £m	*Sheffield* £m	*Birmingham* £m
Turnover	3.10	2.60	2.75
Cost of sales	1.48	0.91	0.96
Gross profit	1.62	1.69	1.79
Administration cost	0.15	0.17	0.18
Distribution cost	0.45	0.40	0.40
	0.60	0.57	0.58
Net profit	1.02	1.12	1.21

During the year North Notts had sold goods (at cost) for £0.26m and £0.41m respectively to the Sheffield and Birmingham units.

Capital employed	£5.9m	£4.4m	£4.5m
Number of full-time equivalent employees	25	20	22
Wages and salaries included in costs above	£340,000	£290,000	£313,500

LONDON SPORTS SUPPLIES LTD

Four year review of performance

Years	*20X1* £m	*20X2* £m	*20X3* £m	*20X4* £m
Turnover	5.25	5.91	6.30	7.10
Cost of sales	2.10	2.24	2.40	2.63
Gross profit	3.15	3.67	3.90	4.47
Administration cost	0.32	0.35	0.38	0.43
Distribution cost	0.84	0.95	1.05	1.10
	1.16	1.30	1.43	1.53
Net profit	1.99	2.37	2.47	2.94
Number of full-time equivalent employees	56	58	60	65
Capital employed (£m)	7.96	9.35	11.01	12.74

LONDON SPORTS SUPPLIES LTD

Price index appropriate to the business sector

20X1	103.50
20X2	106.10
20X3	108.75
20X4	111.68
20X5	114.24

MEMO

To: Accounting Technician

From: Michael Bateman

Date: 27 January 20X6

Subject: Sportswear Supplies Trade Association (SSTA) Inter-firm Comparison

I attach a form recently received from SSTA.

Could you please prepare this for my signature and submission to SSTA; it needs to be returned no later than 28 February.

If you have difficulty with any items on the return, please don't hesitate to contact me.

Many thanks.

Michael

AAT UNIT 7

PRACTICE DEVOLVED ASSESSMENT 4

ANSWER BOOKLET

TASK 1

LONDON SPORTS SUPPLIES LTD

Summary operating statement for year ended 31 December 20X5

£m

Turnover

Cost of sales

_____

Gross profit

_____

Administration costs

Distribution costs

_____

_____

Net profit

_____

TASK 2

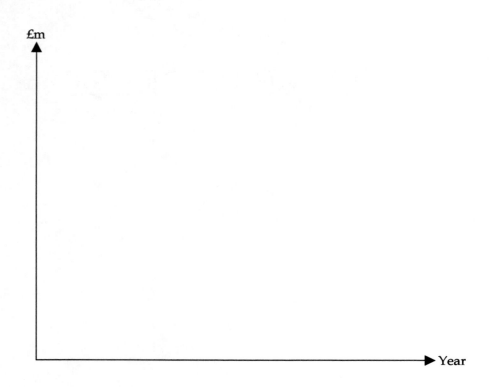

TASK 3

LONDON SPORTS SUPPLIES LTD

Summary of turnover 20X1 – 20X5

Year	20X1 £m	20X2 £m	20X3 £m	20X4 £m	20X5 £m
Actual turnover	5.25	5.91	6.30	7.10	
Price index					
Adjusted turnover to 20X1 prices					

TASK 4

LONDON SPORTS SUPPLIES LTD

Ratio analysis - five year review

	20X1	20X2	Year 20X3	20X4	20X5
Ratio					
Return on capital employed (%)					
Gross profit % of sales					
Net profit % of sales					
Administration costs % of sales					
Distribution costs % of sales					
Turnover per employee					
Capital employed per employee					
Net profit per employee					

(Express the last three ratios to the nearest £000.)

TASK 5

SSTA

Inter-firm comparison scheme 20X5

Business name: ....

Year ended: ....

                                                                                        £m

Turnover

Cost of sales

Gross profit % of sales   ....%

Net profit % of sales   ....%

Administration and distribution costs as % of sales   ....%

Number of full-time equivalent employees

                                                                              _____

Turnover per employee (to nearest £000)   £..................

Wages and salaries per employee (to nearest £000)   £..................

                                                                              _____

Signature: ....

Date: ....

TASK 5 (continued)

LONDON SPORTS SUPPLIES LTD

MEMO

To:

From:

Date:

Subject:

....

....

....

....

....

....

....

....

....

....

....

....

....

....

....

....

....

....

....

....

PRACTICE DEVOLVED ASSESSMENT 5

Daniel and James, Licensed Accounting Technicians

This practice devolved assessment is designed to test your competence in preparing reports and returns.

You will be allowed **1 hour** to prepare your work.

The practice devolved assessment covers the following performance criteria.

Element 3   Prepare VAT returns

Performance criteria

1   VAT returns are correctly completed using data from the appropriate recording systems and are submitted within the statutory time limits.

2   Relevant inputs and outputs are correctly identified and calculated.

3   Submissions are made in accordance with current legislation.

Range statement

1   Recording systems: computerised ledgers; manual control account; cash book.

2   Inputs and outputs: standard supplies; exempt supplies; zero-rated supplies; imports; exports.

Data and tasks

The following pages contain the situation, data and tasks for this assessment. The assessment is divided into two tasks.

You are advised to read the complete file of information before commencing your work.

Documents provided

Schedules and forms to assist you with your tasks are included both below and in the answer booklet.

The situation

Business: Daniel and James, Licensed Accounting Technicians

Personnel: Partners – James Musgrave and Daniel Robb
                          Accounting technician senior – you
                          Junior technician – Brenda Peach
                          Administration assistant – Diane Kelly

DATA AND TASKS

Your work involves bookkeeping and accounting services mainly to small businesses.

Mark Ambrose is one of your clients; he is a self-employed master joiner and this assessment focuses on his file. The time is mid October 20X1.

Tasks to be completed

TASK 1

Refer to the memo from James Musgrave below, immediately following the Tasks, regarding Mark Ambrose, and prepare the VAT form for the quarter ended 30 September 20X1 – a blank VAT form is provided in the answer booklet.

TASK 2

Write a letter to Mark Ambrose enclosing his VAT return for signature and explain to him how you have dealt with the VAT on the bad debts listed on his schedule, and also the private use of the materials.

Write your letter on the blank notepaper provided in the answer booklet.

Data

MEMO

To: Accounting Technician

From: James Musgrave

Date: 15 October 20X1

Subject: Mark Ambrose - VAT return and query

I attach a letter and details relating to Mark's VAT return for quarter ended 30 September 20X1.

Could you please complete the form, incorporating any necessary adjustments for VAT on bad debts queried in his letter.

Many thanks.

James

Mark Ambrose
Master Joiner
High Park House
High Melton
Doncaster   DN5 7EZ

13 October 20X1

Dear James

I attach two schedules you will need for completing my VAT return for this quarter.

I have suffered some loss from bad debts in recent months and would like you to claim back the VAT on these – if that is possible.

I look forward to hearing from you shortly.

Yours sincerely

Mark

MARK AMBROSE

Summary of day books and petty cash expenditure
Quarter ended 30 September 20X1

Sales day book

	Work done £	VAT £	Total £
July	12,900.00	2,257.50	15,157.50
August	13,200.00	2,310.00	15,510.00
September	12,300.00	2,152.50	14,452.50

Purchase day book

	Net £	VAT £	Total £
July	5,250.00	918.75	6,168.75
August	5,470.00	957.25	6,427.25
September	5,750.00	1,006.25	6,756.25

Petty cash expenditure for quarter (VAT inclusive)

July	£105.75
August	£94.00
September	£117.50

I have also used some materials from my stock, valued at £500 (exclusive of VAT), to repair my garage roof.

Bad debts list – 30 September 20X1

Date	Customer	Total (including VAT)
30 November 20X0	High Melton Farms	£293.75
3 January 20X1	Concorde Motors	£176.25
4 April 20X1	Bawtry Engineering	£117.50

These have now been written off as bad debts.

AAT UNIT 7

PRACTICE DEVOLVED ASSESSMENT 5

ANSWER BOOKLET

TASK 1

<table>
<tr><td colspan="2">**Value Added Tax Return**
For the period
01/07/X1 to 30/09/X1</td><td colspan="2">For Official Use</td></tr>
</table>

HM Customs and Excise

Value Added Tax Return

For the period

01/07/X1 to 30/09/X1

For Official Use

Registration number	Period
123 9872 17	09 X1

You could be liable to a financial penalty if your completed return and all the VAT payable are not received by the due date.

Due date: 31.10.X1

For official use

Mark Ambrose
High Park House
High Melton
Doncaster
DN5 7EZ

ATTENTION

If you may trade or pay taxes in euro from Jan 1999, Contact your Business Advice Centre for C&E queries or Treasury Enquiry Unit on 020 7270 4558

Your VAT Office telephone number is 0151 644211

Before you fill in this form read the notes on the back and the VAT leaflet *'Filling in your VAT Return'*. Fill in all boxes clearly in ink, and write 'none' where necessary. Don't put a dash or leave any box blank. If there are no pence write '00' in the pence column. **Do not** enter more than one amount in any box.

For official use			£	p
	VAT due in this period on **sales** and other outputs	1		
	VAT due in this period on **acquisitions** from other **EC Member States**	2		
	Total VAT due **(the sum of boxes 1 and 2)**	3		
	VAT reclaimed in this period on **purchases** and other inputs (including acquisitions from the EC)	4		
	Net VAT to be paid to Customs or reclaimed by you (Difference between boxes 3 and 4)	5		
	Total value of **sales** and all other outputs excluding any VAT. **Include your box 8 figure.**	6		00
	Total value of **purchases** and all other inputs excluding any VAT. **Include your box 9 figure.**	7		00
	Total value of all **supplies** of goods and related services, excl any VAT, to other **EC Member States.**	8		00
	Total value of all **acquisitions** of goods and related servs, excl any VAT, from other **EC Member States.**	9		00

Retail schemes. If you have used any of the schemes in the period covered by this return, enter the relevant letter(s) in this box.

If you are enclosing a payment please tick this box.	DECLARATION: You, or someone on your behalf, must sign below. I, ... declare that the (Full name of signatory in BLOCK LETTERS) information given above is true and complete. Signature... Date .... 20............. **A false declaration can result in prosecution.**

VAT 100 (Full)   0141846

PCU (June 1996)

F

TASK 2

DANIEL AND JAMES

LICENSED ACCOUNTING TECHNICIANS

Stonehill House
Stonehill Rise
Doncaster
DN5 9HB

Tel/Fax: 01302 786050

e-mail: danjames@virgin.net

Partners: James Musgrave FMAAT
Daniel Robb FMAAT

PRACTICE DEVOLVED ASSESSMENT 6
Crescent Hotel

This practice devolved assessment is designed to test your competence in preparing reports and returns.

You will be allowed **1 hour** to complete your work.

The performance criteria covered in this practice devolved assessment are as follows:

Element 3   Prepare VAT returns

Performance criteria

1   VAT returns are correctly completed using data from the appropriate recording systems and are submitted within the statutory time limits.

2   Relevant inputs and outputs are correctly identified and calculated.

3   Submissions are made in accordance with current legislation.

4   Guidance is sought from the VAT office when required, in a professional manner.

Range statement

1   Recording systems: computerised ledgers; manual control account; cash book.

2   Inputs and outputs: standard supplies; exempt supplies; zero-rated supplies; imports; exports.

Data and tasks

The practice devolved assessment is set out on the following pages. The assessment is divided into three tasks.

Documents provided

Schedules and forms to assist you with your tasks are included below and in the answer booklet.

The situation

Business: Simon White – self-employed accounting technician

Location: North East Coast of England

You are to adopt the role of Simon White.

Your work includes a bookkeeping and accounting service to small businesses, particularly small hotels and guesthouses, restaurants and public houses.

One of your clients is Crescent Hotel which has 40 bedrooms, a small restaurant and bar. The hotel is owned by John and Norma Thistle. The time is mid October 20X1 and you are currently working on their bookkeeping and VAT records for the quarter ended 30 September 20X1.

Tasks to be completed

TASK 1

Immediately following these tasks you will find a summary of the records from the day books for the period ended 30 September, together with other relevant notes.

There is also a short note attached from John Thistle regarding a bad debt.

Using the blank VAT form provided in the answer booklet, prepare the return ready for John Thistle's signature.

TASK 2

When you have completed the form, John is not around to see you.

Prepare a note for John explaining briefly how you have adjusted the return to account for the matters brought to your attention. Use the space provided in the answer booklet for your note.

TASK 3

A few days later you receive a phone call from Norma who informs you that she is considering the purchase of a newsagents' shop close to the hotel.

She says that she has heard that special VAT schemes apply to the retail trade.

Before responding fully to her, you decide to write to the VAT office for clarification of the scheme or schemes which apply to this type of business.

Write a letter to the VAT office at:

> Customs House
> Bright Street
> Scarborough
> North Yorkshire
> YO33 23J

regarding this issue. Use the blank notepaper provided in the answer booklet.

Data

CRESCENT HOTEL

Summary of day books for quarter ended 30 September 20X1

Hotel sales day book

	Net £	VAT £	Gross £
July	17,300.00	3,027.50	20,327.50
August	20,200.00	3,535.00	23,735.00
September	17,600.00	3,080.00	20,680.00

Sales - Gross takings in cash

	Bar £	Restaurant £
July	3,877.50	6,873.75
August	4,935.00	6,638.75
September	3,466.25	6,168.75

Purchase day book

		Net £	VAT £	Gross £
July }		5,190.00	908.25	6,098.25
August }	Hotel	6,060.00	1,060.50	7,120.50
September }		5,280.00	924.00	6,204.00
July – September (bar and restaurant)		10,800.00	1,890.00	12,690.00

Petty cash expenditure

Gross for period   £481.75

NOTE

To: Simon

From: John

Date: 16 October 20X1

Simon, you are aware that we had three residents last year (December 20X0) from a company working in the area. This company has now gone into liquidation and we have been informed that we will not receive any funds against this debt.

Could you please, if possible, claim back the VAT from Customs and Excise.

The gross value of the invoice was £587.50.

Also, in mid-August it was Norma's birthday and we 'put on' a surprise party for her. We used £300 worth of stock from the restaurant and the bar.

Do we need to adjust any figures for VAT?

AAT UNIT 7

PRACTICE DEVOLVED ASSESSMENT 6

ANSWER BOOKLET

TASK 1

	Value Added Tax Return	For Official Use	
	For the period		
HM Customs and Excise	**01/07/X1 to 30/09/X1**		

Value Added Tax Return

For the period

01/07/X1 to 30/09/X1

HM Customs and Excise

For Official Use

Registration number	Period
179 6421 27	09 X1

John Thistle
t/as Crescent Hotel
High Street
Whitby
YO21 37L   140784/06

You could be liable to a financial penalty if your completed return and all the VAT payable are not received by the due date.

Due date: 31.10.X1

For official use	

Your VAT Office telephone number is 0151 644211

ATTENTION

If you may trade or pay taxes in euro from Jan 1999, Contact your Business Advice Centre for C&E queries or Treasury Enquiry Unit on 020 7270 4558

Before you fill in this form read the notes on the back and the VAT leaflet *'Filling in your VAT Return'*. Fill in all boxes clearly in ink, and write 'none' where necessary. Don't put a dash or leave any box blank. If there are no pence write '00' in the pence column. **Do not** enter more than one amount in any box.

For official use			£	p
	VAT due in this period on **sales** and other outputs	1		
	VAT due in this period on **acquisitions** from other **EC Member States**	2		
	Total VAT due (**the sum of boxes 1 and 2**)	3		
	VAT reclaimed in this period on **purchases** and other inputs (including acquisitions from the EC)	4		
	Net VAT to be paid to Customs or reclaimed by you (Difference between boxes 3 and 4)	5		
	Total value of **sales** and all other outputs excluding any VAT. **Include your box 8 figure.**	6		00
	Total value of **purchases** and all other inputs excluding any VAT. **Include your box 9 figure.**	7		00
	Total value of all **supplies** of goods and related services, excl any VAT, to other **EC Member States.**	8		00
	Total value of all **acquisitions** of goods and related servs, excl any VAT, from other **EC Member States.**	9		00

Retail schemes. If you have used any of the schemes in the period covered by this return, enter the relevant letter(s) in this box.

If you are enclosing a payment please tick this box.	DECLARATION: You, or someone on your behalf, must sign below.

I, ... declare that the
(Full name of signatory in BLOCK LETTERS)
information given above is true and complete.
Signature.. Date ....20.............
A false declaration can result in prosecution.

VAT 100 (Full)   0141846

PCU (June 1996)

F

TASK 2

NOTE

To: John Thistle

From: Simon White

Date: 18 October 20X1

....

....

....

....

....

....

....

....

....

....

....

....

....

....

....

....

....

....

....

....

....

....

....

TASK 3

Simon White FMAAT
Accounting Technician
Bay Farm
High Street
Hawsker
YO21 3EJ

Date: ....

....

....

....

....

....

....

....

....

....

....

....

....

....

....

....

....

....

....

....

....

....

....

MOCK DEVOLVED ASSESSMENT 1
(AAT Sample Simulation)

DATA AND TASKS

Instructions

This practice devolved assessment is designed to test your ability to prepare reports and returns.

The situation and the tasks to be performed are set out below.

The practice devolved assessment also contains a large volume of data which you will require in order to complete the tasks.

Your answers should be set out in the answer booklet, using the answer sheets provided.

You are allowed **three** hours to complete your work.

A high level of accuracy is required. Check your work before handing it in.

Correcting fluid may be used but it should be used in moderation. Errors should be crossed out neatly and clearly. You should write in black ink, not pencil.

The information you require is provided as far as possible in the sequence in which you will need to deal with it. However, you are advised to look quickly through all the material before you begin. This will help you to familiarise yourself with the situation and the information available.

The situation

Your name is Sol Bellcamp and you work as an accounts assistant for a printing company, Hoddle Limited. Hoddle Limited is owned 100% by another printing company, Kelly Limited. You report to the Group Accountant, Sherry Teddingham.

Hoddle Limited manufactures a wide range of printed materials such as cards, brochures and booklets. Most customers are based in the UK, but sales are also made to other countries in the European Union (EU). There are no exports to countries outside the EU. All of the company's purchases come from businesses within the UK.

Hoddle Limited is registered for VAT and it makes both standard-rated and zero-rated supplies to its UK customers. All sales to other EU countries qualify as zero-rated. The company's local VAT office is at Brendon House, 14 Abbey Street, Pexley PY2 3WR.

Kelly Limited is separately registered for VAT; there is no group registration in force. Both companies have an accounting year ending on 31 March. There are no other companies in the Kelly group.

Hoddle Limited is a relatively small company and sometimes suffers from shortage of capacity to complete customers' jobs. In these cases, the printing work is done by Kelly Limited. Kelly then sells the completed products to Hoddle for onward sale to the customer. The sale from Kelly to Hoddle is recorded in the books of each company at cost; Kelly does not charge a profit margin.

In this practice devolved assessment you are concerned with the accounting year ended 31 March 20X8.

♦ To begin with you will be required to prepare the VAT return for Hoddle Limited in respect of the quarter ended 31 March 20X8.

♦ You will then be required to prepare certain reports, both for internal use and for an external inter-firm comparison scheme, covering the whole accounting year ended 31 March 20X8. These reports will treat the two companies as a single group; they will contain consolidated figures, not figures for either of the two companies separately.

Today's date is 9 April 20X8.

Tasks to be completed

TASK 1

Refer to the three invoices immediately following these tasks, which have been received from Hoddle Ltd's suppliers during March 20X8. No entries have yet been made in Hoddle Ltd's books of account in respect of these documents. You are required to explain how you will treat each one of these documents when preparing Hoddle Ltd's VAT return for the period January to March 20X8. Set out your answer in the space provided in the answer booklet.

TASK 2

Refer to the sales day book summary, purchases day book summary, cash book summary and petty cash book summary in the data below. These have been printed out from Hoddle Ltd's computerised accounting system for the period January to March 20X8. (You are reminded that these summaries do not include the documents dealt with in Task 1.) Refer also to the memo dated 6 April in the data below. Using this information you are required to complete the VAT return of Hoddle Ltd for the quarter ended 31 March 20X8. A blank return is provided for this purpose in the answer booklet.

TASK 3

The Group Accountant is considering adoption of the cash accounting scheme for VAT. He believes that Hoddle Ltd (though not Kelly Ltd) might qualify for the scheme. He has asked you to draft a letter to the VAT office, in his name, requesting certain details of the scheme. He is interested in the turnover limit for the scheme, particularly since Hoddle is a member of a group of companies, and in the effect of the scheme in dealing with bad debts. Draft a letter in the space provided in the answer booklet.

TASK 4

Refer to the profit and loss account of Kelly Ltd in the data below which covers the period 1 January to 31 March 20X8. You are required to prepare a profit and loss account for the same period in which the results of Hoddle and Kelly are consolidated. Prepare your answer as follows, using the schedule provided in the answer booklet.

♦ Enter the results of Kelly in the first column.

♦ Using the information already provided for earlier tasks, construct the results of Hoddle Ltd and enter them in the second column. Note that Hoddle Ltd's stock at 1 January 20X8 was valued at £14,638, while stock at 31 March 20X8 was valued at £16,052.

♦ Make appropriate adjustments in the third column to eliminate the effects of trading between Kelly and Hoddle.

♦ Calculate the consolidated figures and enter them in the fourth column.

TASK 5

Refer to the consolidated balance sheet, schedule of quarterly consolidated profit and loss accounts, and the memo dated 2 April in the data below. Using these, and the information already provided for earlier tasks, you are required to prepare a report for the accountant on the group results for the year ended 31 March 20X8. Your report should contain the following:

♦ Key ratios: gross profit margin; net profit margin; return on *shareholders* capital employed.

♦ Sales revenue for each quarter, both in actual terms and indexed to a common base.

♦ A pie chart showing the proportion of annual (unindexed) sales earned in each quarter.

Note: You are not required to comment on the results for the year, merely to present them according to the instructions above. Use the space provided in the answer booklet.

TASK 6

You are required to complete an inter-firm comparison as set out in the answer booklet.

TASK 7

You are required to prepare a memo to the Group Accountant enclosing the inter-firm comparison for authorisation before dispatch. Use the space provided in the answer booklet.

Data

Engineering Supplies Limited
Haddlefield Road, Blaysley, CG6 6AW
Tel/Fax: 01376 44531

Hoddle Limited
22 Formguard Street
Pexley
PY6 3QW

SALES INVOICE NO: 2155

Date: 27 March 20X8

	£
VAT omitted in error from invoice no 2139	
£2,667.30 @ 17.5%	466.77
Total due	466.77

Terms: net 30 days

VAT registration: 318 1827 58

Alpha Stationery

Aindsale Centre, Mexton, EV1 4DF
Telephone: 01392 43215

26 March 20X8

1 box transparent folders : red

Total incl VAT @ 17.5%	14.84
Amount tendered	20.00
Change	5.16

VAT registration: 356 7612 33

JAMIESON & CO

Jamieson House, Baines Road, Gresham, GM7 2PQ
Telephone: 01677 35567   Fax: 01677 57640

PROFORMA SALES INVOICE

VAT registration: 412 7553 67

Hoddle Limited
22 Formguard Street
Pexley
PY6 3QW

For professional services in connection with debt collection	£
Our fees	350.00
VAT	61.25
Total due	411.25

A VAT invoice will be submitted when the total due is paid in full.

HODDLE LIMITED : SALES DAY BOOK SUMMARY

JANUARY TO MARCH 20X8

	JAN £	FEB £	MAR £	TOTAL £
UK: ZERO-RATED	20,091.12	22,397.00	23,018.55	65,506.67
UK: STANDARD-RATED	15,682.30	12,914.03	15,632.98	44,229.31
OTHER EU	874.12	4,992.66	5,003.82	10,870.60
VAT	2,744.40	2,259.95	2,735.77	7,740.12
TOTAL	39,391.94	42,563.64	46,391.12	128,346.70

HODDLE LIMITED : PURCHASES DAY BOOK SUMMARY

JANUARY TO MARCH 20X8

	JAN £	FEB £	MAR £	TOTAL £
PURCHASES	14,532.11	20,914.33	15,461.77	50,908.21*
DISTRIBUTION EXPENSES	4,229.04	3,761.20	5,221.43	13,211.67
ADMIN EXPENSES	5,123.08	2,871.45	3,681.62	11,676.15
OTHER EXPENSES	1,231.00	1,154.99	997.65	3,383.64
VAT	4,027.97	4,543.22	4,119.34	12,690.53
TOTAL	29,143.20	33,245.19	29,481.81	91,870.20

*This figure includes £18,271 of purchases from Kelly Limited.

HODDLE LIMITED : CASH BOOK SUMMARY

JANUARY TO MARCH 20X8

	JAN £	FEB £	MAR £	TOTAL £
PAYMENTS:				
TO CREDITORS	12,901.37	15,312.70	18,712.44	46,926.51
TO PETTY CASH	601.40	555.08	623.81	1,780.29
WAGES/SALARIES	5,882.18	6,017.98	6,114.31	18,014.47
TOTAL	19,384.95	21,885.76	25,450.56	66,721.27
RECEIPTS:				
VAT FROM CUSTOMS AND EXCISE	2,998.01			2,998.01
FROM CUSTOMERS	29,312.44	34,216.08	36,108.77	99,637.29
TOTAL	32,310.45	34,216.08	36,108.77	102,635.30
SURPLUS FOR MONTH	12,925.50	12,330.32	10,658.21	
BALANCE B/F	-8,712.41	4,213.09	16,543.41	
BALANCE C/F	4,213.09	16,543.41	27,201.62	

HODDLE LIMITED : PETTY CASH BOOK SUMMARY

JANUARY TO MARCH 20X8

	JAN £	FEB £	MAR £	TOTAL £
PAYMENTS:				
STATIONERY	213.85	80.12	237.58	531.55
TRAVEL	87.34	76.50	102.70	266.54
OFFICE EXPENSES	213.66	324.08	199.51	737.25
VAT	86.55	74.38	84.02	244.95
TOTAL	601.40	555.08	623.81	1,780.29
RECEIPTS:				
FROM CASH BOOK	601.40	555.08	623.81	1,780.29
SURPLUS FOR MONTH	0.00	0.00	0.00	
BALANCE B/F	200.00	200.00	200.00	
BALANCE C/F	200.00	200.00	200.00	

MEMO

To: Sol Bellcamp

From: Sherry Teddingham

Date: 6 April 20X8

Subject: Bad debt – Batty Limited

As you probably know, we have had great difficulty in persuading the above customer to pay what he owes us. We invoiced him in July 20X7 for £420 plus VAT at the standard rate, but he has always disputed the debt and it looks as though we will never recover it. We wrote it off to the bad debt account in March of this year, so you should take this into account when preparing the VAT return for the quarter just ended.

Kelly Limited
Profit and loss account for the three months ended 31 March 20X8

	£	£
Sales to external customers		275,601
Sales to Hoddle Limited at cost		20,167*
Total sales		295,768
Opening stock	28,341	
Purchases	136,095	
	164,436	
Closing stock	31,207	
Cost of sales		133,229
Gross profit		162,539
Wages and salaries	47,918	
Distribution expenses	28,341	
Administration expenses	30,189	
Stationery	2,541	
Travel	2,001	
Office expenses	3,908	
Interest payable	12,017	
Other expenses	11,765	
		138,680
Net profit for the period		23,859

*This figure includes £1,896 in respect of a job completed on 31 March 20X8 but not delivered to Hoddle Limited until 1 April 20X8. It is not included in Hoddle Ltd's purchases for the period ended 31 March.

Kelly and Hoddle
Consolidated balance sheet at 31 March 20X8

	£	£
Fixed assets at net book value		1,229,348
Current assets		
Stock	49,155	
Trade debtors	223,009	
VAT recoverable	13,451	
Cash at bank and in hand	40,088	
	325,703	
Current liabilities		
Trade creditors	136,531	
Other creditors	11,740	
	148,271	
Net current assets		177,432
Total assets less current liabilities		1,406,780
Long-term liability		
Loan repayable in 20Y4		372,072
		1,034,708
Capital and reserves		
Called up share capital		234,167
Retained profits		800,541
		1,034,708

Quarterly consolidated profit and loss accounts
for the year ended 31 March 20X8

	1 Apr X7 to 30 Jun X7 £	1 Jul X7 to 30 Sep X7 £	1 Oct X7 to 31 Dec X7 £	1 Jan X8 to 31 Mar X8 £	*Totals for year* 1 Apr X7 to 31 Mar X8 £
Sales	325,719	275,230	306,321		
Cost of sales	134,861	109,421	121,358		
Gross profit	190,858	165,809	184,963		
Wages and salaries	63,314	61,167	64,412		
Distribution expenses	34,217	30,135	31,221		
Admin expenses	34,765	33,012	36,415		
Stationery	2,981	2,671	3,008		
Travel	1,975	1,876	2,413		
Office expenses	4,412	4,713	3,083		
Interest payable	12,913	12,714	12,432		
Other expenses	10,981	16,421	15,431		
	165,558	162,709	168,415		
Net profit for the period	25,300	3,100	16,548		

Note for candidates: you are advised to complete the above schedule by filling in the figures for the final quarter in the fourth column and totalling the figures for the year in the final column.

MEMO

To: Sol Bellcamp

From: Sherry Teddingham

Date: 2 April 20X8

Subject: Adjusting for the effects of price rises

When presenting your quarterly reports on group results please include an item of information additional to that which you normally present. As well as noting sales revenue by quarter, please present quarterly sales revenue adjusted to take account of price rises.

I have identified a suitable index as follows:

First quarter 20X6/X7 (base period)	231.8
First quarter 20X7/X8	239.3
Second quarter 20X7/X8	241.5
Third quarter 20X7/X8	244.0
Fourth quarter 20X7/X8	241.8

I will keep you informed of future movements in this index.

AAT UNIT 7

MOCK DEVOLVED ASSESSMENT 1

ANSWER BOOKLET

TASK 1

TASK 2

	Value Added Tax Return	For Official Use

Value Added Tax Return

For the period
01/01/X8 to 31/03/X8

HM Customs
and Excise

For Official Use

Registration number | Period
578 4060 19 | 03 X8

081 578 4060 19 100 03 98
235192
Mr Sherry Teddingham
Hoddle Limited
22 Formguard Street
Pexley   PY6 3ZW   219921/10

Fold Here

You could be liable to a financial penalty
if your completed return and all the
VAT payable are not received by the
due date.

Due date: 30 04 X8

For
official
use
D O R
only

Before you fill in this form read the notes on the back and the VAT leaflet *'Filling in your VAT Return'*. Fill in all boxes clearly in ink, and write 'none' where necessary. Don't put a dash or leave any box blank. If there are no pence write '00' in the pence column. **Do not** enter more than one amount in any box.

For official use			£	p
	VAT due in this period on **sales** and other outputs	1		
	VAT due in this period on **acquisitions** from other **EC Member States**	2		
	Total VAT due (**the sum of boxes 1 and 2**)	3		
	VAT reclaimed in this period on **purchases** and other inputs (including acquisitions from the EC)	4		
	Net VAT to be paid to Customs or reclaimed by you (Difference between boxes 3 and 4)	5		
	Total value of **sales** and all other outputs excluding any VAT. **Include your box 8 figure.**	6		00
	Total value of **purchases** and all other inputs excluding any VAT. **Include your box 9 figure.**	7		00
	Total value of all **supplies** of goods and related services, excl any VAT, to other **EC Member States.**	8		00
	Total value of all **acquisitions** of goods and related servs, excl any VAT, from other **EC Member States.**	9		00

Retail schemes. If you have used any of the schemes in the period covered by this return, enter the relevant letter(s) in this box.

If you are enclosing a payment please tick this box.	DECLARATION: You, or someone on your behalf, must sign below.

I, ………………………………………………………………....……….. declare that the
(Full name of signatory in BLOCK LETTERS)
information given above is true and complete.
Signature………………………………….. Date ………………………. 20………….

A false declaration can result in prosecution.

VAT 100 (Full)   PCU (June 1996)

TASK 3

Hoddle Limited
22 Formguard Street, Pexley, PY6 3QW
Telephone 01682 431256

....

....

....

....

....

....

....

....

....

....

....

....

....

....

....

....

....

....

....

....

....

....

Registered office: 22 Formguard Street, Pexley, PY6 3QW
Registered in England, number 2314561

TASK 4

Consolidated profit and loss account
for the three months ended 31 March 20X8

	Kelly £	Hoddle £	Adjustments £	Consolidated £
Sales				
	———	———	———	———
Opening stock				
Purchases				
	———	———	———	———
Closing stock				
	———	———	———	———
Cost of sales				
	———	———	———	———
	———	———	———	———
Gross profit				
	———	———	———	———
Wages and salaries				
Distribution expenses				
Administration expenses				
Stationery				
Travel				
Office expenses				
Interest payable				
Other expenses				
	———	———		———
	———	———		———
	———	———		———
Net profit for the period				
	———	———		———

TASK 5

TASK 6

Inter-firm comparison data (extracts)

Name of company ....

Year ended ....

Data

	£	% of sales	Industry best	Industry average
Sales				
Gross profit			62.1%	57.3%
Net profit			10.4%	5.8%
Fixed assets				
Current assets				
Current liabilities				
Return on capital employed			10.3%	9.0%

Important note

Before completing this form you should read the explanatory notes below

Note 1

'Sales' means sales to external customers. Inter-company, inter-divisional or inter-branch sales should be excluded.

Note 2

Fixed assets should be stated at net book value.

Note 3

Return on capital employed is net profit before interest charges, divided by capital employed.

TASK 7

MOCK DEVOLVED ASSESSMENT 2
Houillier Ltd

DATA AND TASKS

Instructions

This practice devolved assessment is designed to test your ability to prepare reports and returns.

The situation and the tasks to be completed are set out below.

The practice devolved assessment also contains data which you will require in order to complete the tasks.

Your answers should be set out in the answer booklet, using the answer sheets provided. If you require additional answer pages, ask the person in charge.

You are allowed **three hours** to complete your work.

A high level of accuracy is required. Check your work before handing it in.

Correcting fluid may be used, but it should be used in moderation. Errors should be crossed out neatly and clearly. You should write in black ink, not pencil.

The information you require is provided as far as possible in the sequence in which you will need to deal with it. However, you are advised to look quickly through all of the material before you begin. This will help you to familiarise yourself with the situation and the information available.

You are reminded that you should not bring any unauthorised material, such as books or notes, into the practice devolved assessment. If you have any such material in your possession, you should surrender it to the assessor immediately.

Any instances of misconduct will be brought to the attention of the AAT, and disciplinary action may be taken.

Coverage of performance criteria and range statements

It should be recognised that it is not always possible to cover all performance criteria and range statements in a practice devolved assessment; some may be more appropriate and entirely natural in the workplace and others may not be practicable within the scope of a particular practice devolved assessment. Where performance criteria and range statements are not covered they must be assessed by other means by the assessor before a candidate can be deemed competent. A schedule at the end of the data below gives an indication of the performance criteria coverage for this practice devolved assessment and also flags up the need to ensure that all areas of the range statement are covered.

The situation

Your name is Stevie Real and you work as an accounts assistant for Houillier Limited, a wholesaling company based in Liverpool. Operations are conducted through two outlets: the City Centre branch and the District branch. Along with all other office staff in Houillier you work in office accommodation housed in the City Centre branch. You report to Janice Knapper, the accounts supervisor.

Houillier's most recent accounting period is the year ended 30 September 20X9. Part of the work facing you at the moment is to prepare consolidated information relating to costs and revenues arising in that year. ('Consolidated' information means total information relating to the two branches combined.)

Houillier is a member of the Federation of North Western Wholesalers (FNWW), a trade body. Members of FNWW submit an annual report to the Federation which includes summarised financial information. The Federation uses this to prepare comparative information for use by members. The second main task on your agenda at present is to complete the annual report ready for submission to FNWW.

Finally, you are also responsible for preparing the company's VAT return. The return for the quarter ended 30 September 20X9 is to be prepared in good time for submission to Customs and Excise by 31 October 20X9.

In relation to VAT, Houillier's sales to UK customers are all standard-rated. All sales to other EU countries qualify as zero-rated. The company's local VAT office is at 38 Bergerac Road, Babbtown, Liverpool, L16 3NV. The company settles its quarterly VAT liability by enclosing a cheque along with its VAT 100 return.

Tasks to be completed

TASK 1

Immediately following the tasks below, you will find cost and revenue data for the year ended 30 September 20X9 for both the City Centre branch and the District Branch (a profit and loss account and other information for each).

You are required to consolidate this information (ie combine the information for the two branches) so as to produce a profit and loss account for the company as a whole for the year ended 30 September 20X9. Note that transfers between the two branches are not to be treated as sales or purchases and must instead be excluded from the consolidated figures.

Use the proforma provided in the answer booklet to set out your answer.

TASK 2

Reproduced in the answer booklet you will find the company's consolidated profit and loss account for the year ended 30 September 20X8. A price index appropriate to the company had an average value of 161.2 during year ended 30 September 20X8 and an average value of 168.8 during year ended 30 September 20X9.

You are required to restate the 20X8 profit and loss account in terms of 20X9 prices using the average values of the price index given above, and to show the percentage change from 20X8 (restated) to 20X9 in each line of the profit and loss account. Your calculations of the percentage should be accurate to one decimal place. (You may find it helpful to enter the 20X9 figures calculated in Task 1 on the schedule provided for Task 2 in the answer booklet.)

TASK 3

You are required to write a memo, dated 11 October 20X9, to your accounts supervisor.

In the memo you should:

(a)   set out the following ratios for the year ended 30 September 20X9:

  ♦   gross profit margin

  ♦   net profit margin

  ♦   return on capital employed (the average capital employed by Houillier Limited during the year ended 30 September 20X9 was £21,600,000).

(b)   include a pie chart showing the total sales revenue for the year broken down into slices for:

  ♦   cost of goods sold

  ♦   wholesaling wages and salaries

  ♦   administration wages and salaries

  ♦   other costs

  ♦   net profit.

Your pie chart should clearly indicate the percentage of sales revenue represented by each of these items.

Use the blank memo form provided in the answer booklet.

(This task relates entirely to the *consolidated* results for 20X8/X9, ie the results for the two branches combined, not to the results of each branch singly.)

TASK 4

You are required to enter the relevant details on the FNWW annual report set out in the answer booklet. You should then send a memo dated 12 October 1999, enclosing the completed form for the attention and approval of your accounts supervisor prior to its despatch to FNWW. Use the blank memo form provided in the answer booklet.

TASK 5

Refer to the sales day book summary, purchases day book summary, and petty cash book summary in the data below. Using this information you are required to complete the VAT return of Houillier Limited for the quarter ended 30 September 20X9 ready for signature by the accounts supervisor. A blank VAT return is provided in the answer booklet.

TASK 6

Your accounts supervisor believes that the company may be eligible to account for VAT using the special schemes designed for retail businesses. You are required to draft a letter to your local VAT office requesting details of these schemes. Use the blank letterhead provided in the answer booklet and date your letter 12 October 20X9.

Data

CITY CENTRE BRANCH

Profit and loss account for the year ended 30 September 20X9

	£	£
Sales to external customers		8,672,130
Transfers to District branch (valued at cost)		387,160
		9,059,290
Opening stock	934,120	
Purchases	6,521,540	
	7,455,660	
Less closing stock	1,065,410	
Cost of goods sold		6,390,250
Gross profit		2,669,040
Wholesaling wages and salaries*	856,120	
Administration wages and salaries**	549,780	
Other costs	574,000	
		1,979,900
Net profit for the year		689,140

*   Average number of employees (full-time equivalents) = 79
** Average number of employees (full-time equivalents) = 41

Note: A consignment of goods, costing £26,550, was despatched to the District branch on 30 September 20X9, but was not recorded in District's stock until 1 October 20X9.

DISTRICT BRANCH

Profit and loss account for the year ended 30 September 20X9

	£	£
Sales to external customers		6,241,100
Opening stock	518,710	
Purchases	4,111,900	
Transfers from City Centre branch at cost	360,610	
	4,991,220	
Less closing stock	597,230	
Cost of goods sold		4,393,990
Gross profit		1,847,110
Wholesaling wages and salaries*	801,980	
Other costs	423,170	
		1,225,150
Net profit for the year		621,960

* Average number of employees (full-time equivalents) = 71

Note: A consignment of goods, from the City Centre branch, despatched on 30 September 20X9, was not recorded in District's stock until 1 October 20X9. The cost of these goods was £26,550.

HOUILLIER LIMITED

Sales day book summary – July to September 20X9

	July £	August £	September £	Total £
UK: STANDARD RATED	890,543	912,453	798,125	2,601,121
OTHER EU	100,871	123,009	98,137	322,017
VAT	155,845	159,679	139,672	455,196
TOTAL	1,147,259	1,195,141	1,035,934	3,378,334

HOUILLIER LIMITED

Purchases day book summary – July to September 20X9

	July £	August £	September £	Total £
PURCHASES	781,235	861,200	900,125	2,542,560
OTHER COSTS	68,901	76,432	77,988	223,321
VAT	133,608	150,005	155,432	439,045
TOTAL	983,744	1,087,637	1,133,545	3,204,926

HOUILLIER LIMITED

Petty cash book payments – July to September 20X9

	July £	August £	September £	Total £
OTHER COSTS	1,237	1,509	1,180	3,926
VAT	201	249	188	638
TOTAL	1,438	1,758	1,368	4,564

AAT UNIT 7

MOCK DEVOLVED ASSESSMENT 2

ANSWER BOOKLET

TASK 1

**Consolidated profit and loss account
for the year ended 30 September 20X9**

	City Centre £	District £	Consolidated £
Sales to external customers			
	_____	_____	_____
Opening stock			
Purchases			
Less closing stock			
	_____	_____	_____
Cost of goods sold			
	_____	_____	_____
Gross profit			
Wholesaling wages and salaries			
Administration wages and salaries			
Other costs			
	_____	_____	_____
Net profit for the year			
	_____	_____	_____

TASK 2

**Consolidated profit and loss account
for the years ended 30 September 20X8/20X9**

	20X8 (actual) £	20X8 (restated) £	20X9 £	Change in year %
Sales to external customers	12,247,318			
	_____	_____	_____	_____
Opening stock	1,225,671			
Purchases	9,206,783			
	_____	_____	_____	_____
	10,432,454			
Less closing stock	1,452,830			
	_____	_____	_____	_____
Cost of goods sold	8,979,624			
	_____	_____	_____	_____
Gross profit	3,267,694			
Wholesaling wages and salaries	(1,236,519)			
Administration wages and salaries	(483,512)			
Other costs	(852,090)			
	_____	_____	_____	_____
Net profit for the year	695,573			
	_____	_____	_____	_____

TASK 3

MEMO

To:

From:

Date:

Subject:

....

....

....

....

....

....

....

....

....

....

....

....

....

....

....

....

....

....

....

....

....

....

....

....

TASK 3 (continued)

TASK 4

FEDERATION OF NORTH WESTERN WHOLESALERS

Annual report to be completed by members (extract)

Please supply the information requested below as soon as possible after the end of your accounting period. The ratios and statistics should be calculated in accordance with the conventions and definitions explained in the notes.

Name of member .... Year end ....

Gross margin (Note 2) ....

Net margin (Note 3) ....

Return on capital employed (Note 4) ....

Total of direct salaries (Note 5) ....

Total of indirect salaries (Note 6) ....

Average salary per employee (Note 7) ....

Notes

1 All ratios and statistics should be calculated to one decimal place. Monetary amounts should be stated to the nearest thousand pounds. Members trading through more than one branch or division should submit consolidated information only, ie information for all branches combined as a single entity.

2 Gross margin is the ratio of gross profit to sales, expressed as a percentage.

3 Net margin is the ratio of net profit to sales, expressed as a percentage.

4 Return on capital employed is the ratio of net profit to average capital employed during the accounting period, expressed as a percentage.

5 Direct salaries are those of staff engaged directly in wholesaling activities.

6 Indirect salaries are those of all other staff, including administration staff.

7 Average salary per employee is the total wages and salaries for the year, divided by the number of full-time equivalent staff employed during the year.

TASK 4 (continued)

MEMO

To:

From:

Date:

Subject:

....

....

....

....

....

....

....

....

....

....

....

....

....

....

....

....

....

....

....

....

TASK 5

Value Added Tax Return

For the period

01/07/X9 to 30/09/X9

HM Customs
and Excise

081 578 4060 19 100 09 99   Q41268
HOUILLIER LIMITED
39 CARRAGHER ROAD
JAMESTOWN
LIVERPOOL
L15 3NP   140784/06

Your VAT Office telephone number is 0151 644211

For Official Use

Registration number	Period
578 4060 19	09 X9

You could be liable to a financial penalty if your completed return and all the VAT payable are not received by the due date.

Due date: 31.10.X9

For official use	

ATTENTION

If you may trade or pay taxes in euro from Jan 1999, contact your Business Advice Centre for C&E queries or Treasury Enquiry Unit on 020 7270 4558

Before you fill in this form read the notes on the back and the VAT leaflet *'Filling in your VAT Return'*. Fill in all boxes clearly in ink, and write 'none' where necessary. Don't put a dash or leave any box blank. If there are no pence write '**00**' in the pence column. **Do not** enter more than one amount in any box.

For official use			£	p
	VAT due in this period on **sales** and other outputs	1		
	VAT due in this period on **acquisitions** from other **EC Member States**	2		
	Total VAT due (**the sum of boxes 1 and 2**)	3		
	VAT reclaimed in this period on **purchases** and other inputs (including acquisitions from the EC)	4		
	Net VAT to be paid to Customs or reclaimed by you (Difference between boxes 3 and 4)	5		
	Total value of **sales** and all other outputs excluding any VAT. **Include your box 8 figure.**	6		00
	Total value of **purchases** and all other inputs excluding any VAT. **Include your box 9 figure.**	7		00
	Total value of all **supplies** of goods and related services, excl any VAT, to other **EC Member States.**	8		00
	Total value of all **acquisitions** of goods and related servs, excl any VAT, from other **EC Member States.**	9		00

Retail schemes. If you have used any of the schemes in the period covered by this return, enter the relevant letter(s) in this box.

If you are enclosing a payment please tick this box.	DECLARATION: You, or someone on your behalf, must sign below.
	I, ...……........... declare that the
	(Full name of signatory in BLOCK LETTERS)
	information given above is true and complete.
	Signature... Date .... 20.............
	A false declaration can result in prosecution.

0141846

VAT 100 (Full)   PCU (June 1996)   **F**

TASK 6

HOUILLIER LIMITED

39 Carragher Road, Jamestown, Liverpool, L15 3NP

Telephone: 0151 623 4671

....

....

....

....

....

....

....

....

....

....

....

....

....

....

....

....

....

....

....

....

....

....

Registered in England. Registration number 2314567

AAT UNIT 7

PREPARING REPORTS
AND RETURNS

ANSWERS

KEY TECHNIQUES – ANSWERS

1   Internal and external reports

Answer 1.1

♦ Regular reports are those which relate to a cycle of activities. The weekly analysis of payroll and labour cost (both direct and indirect) to cost centres is an example of a regular report.

♦ Exception reports are prepared to highlight some unusual occurrence. For example, if during a winter period a 'flu' epidemic occurred, then reporting on sick leave and hours lost could form the basis of an exception report.

♦ Analysis is the examination and carrying out of further work on balances and trends in order to gain a better understanding. The reporting and analysis of labour productivity and efficiency per cost centre is an example of such a report.

♦ Forecasts are projections of future activity for expense centres, profit centres and investment centres. These form the basis of forward looking plans, both in terms of short-term budgets and longer-term strategy. A business would prepare a forecast of employee numbers required in six months time in order to ensure that sufficient new employees were recruited before they were required.

♦ The manpower strategy would take the form of a manpower plan.

2   Collecting and organising information

Answer 2.1

The principles of good form design include:

(a)   Requirements must be clearly explained and unambiguous.

  ♦ Terminology must be standardised.
  ♦ Order of completion must be logical.
  ♦ Calculations must be clearly explained.
  ♦ Level of accuracy, eg to nearest '£', must be stated.

(b)   The amount of writing should be kept to a minimum.

  ♦ As much information as possible should be pre-printed.
  ♦ Use boxes to be ticked for a choice of answers.

(c)   The destination of the completed form should be clearly indicated.

  ♦ The name and address of the department or person to whom the form is to be returned should be clearly shown.

(d)   The information requested must be in a format that is easy to process.

  ♦ To facilitate computer analysis of responses.

  ♦ If judgements are required then a range of responses to questions should be included.

(e)   The form should be uniquely identifiable from others.

  ♦ Include title, and colour code the form.

Answer 2.2

General digests would include:

- Monthly Digest of Statistics.

- Annual Abstract of Statistics.

- Social Trends.

Specific digests would include:

- Economic Trends.

- British Business (DTI).

- Employment Gazette.

- National accounts.

- Overseas trade statistics.

- New earnings survey.

3   *Writing reports*

Answer 3.1

REPORT

To:	Managing Director
From:	Accounting Technician
Date:	X – X - XX
Subject:	Inter-firm comparison - agricultural feeds sector

Introduction

We have recently received the following summary from the trade association inter-firm comparison scheme.

Agricultural feeds sector		
Ratio	*Company*	*Industry average*
Return on capital employed	26%	24%
Asset turnover	1.63	1.6
% net profit to sales	16%	15%
Current ratio	1.3 : 1	1.2 : 1
Acid test	0.99 : 1	1.01 : 1

Return on capital employed

The return on capital employed is the primary profitability ratio. It is expressed as:

$$\frac{\text{Net profit before interest and tax}}{\text{Capital employed}} \times 100\%$$

It represents, in percentage terms, the amount of profit being generated from the capital base in the company.

Our current return is slightly higher than that of the industry as a whole as we are generating more profit per '£' of capital employed than our major competitors.

It can be said that we are more profitable.

Asset turnover

This is a measure of how well the company is utilising its assets. It represents the volume of sales achieved in relation to the capital employed in the business.

It is expressed as:

$$\frac{\text{Turnover}}{\text{Capital employed}} = \text{Number of times}$$

We are generating £1.63 in the form of turnover (ie sales exclusive of VAT) for each £1 invested in net assets.

The industry has a ratio of 1.6, so our volume of activity, in relation to capital invested, is slightly greater than our competitors.

We are utilising our assets to a greater capacity.

% net profit to sales

This represents, in percentage terms, the net profit in relation to sales. It is the profit margin.

We have a return of 16% on sales compared with an industry average of 15%.

It may be that our sales mix is more profitable or that we are controlling our other operating costs more effectively than the industry as a whole.

Current ratio

This is a measure of liquidity and is expressed as:

Current assets : Current liabilities

We currently have £1.30 in the form of current assets (ie cash, or other assets to be turned into cash in the near future) to each £1 worth of current liabilities (ie debts due to be paid in the near future).

This means that in the short-run the company should be able to meet its demands from creditors.

This is marginally better than the industry figure of 1.2.

Acid test

This is a stricter test of liquidity as it eliminates stocks from the current ratio calculation; stocks take time to convert to cash. The acid test ratio is expressed as:

(Current assets – Stocks) : Current liabilities

Our ratio is 0.99 : 1, ideally in the short-run this should be around 1 : 1. We see that both our ratio and the industry average ratio are close to this figure.

In the short-term we can meet the demands from creditors.

Conclusion

Our return on capital employed is greater than our competitors as is the asset turnover and profit margin.

We are therefore considered to be more profitable than the industry as a whole.

Our liquidity position is strong and compares well with the sector average.

4 Basic processing of data

Answer 4.1

Stainsacre Park

The smallest value in the distribution is 515, the largest value is 565. The range is therefore 50.

The classes can be grouped as:

(a)

Group	Tally	Frequency
515 but less than 520	111	3
520 but less than 525	111	3
525 but less than 530	̶1̶1̶1̶1̶ 1	6
530 but less than 535	11	2
535 but less than 540	1111	4
540 but less than 545	11	2
545 but less than 550	11	2
550 but less than 555	11	2
555 but less than 560	111	3
560 but less than 565	111	3
565 but less than 570	1	1
		⎯
		31
		⎯

(b) The median value ($\frac{n+1}{2}$ = 16th item) is the 16th item when the items are ranked in order.

Median = 535 visitors

$$\text{Mean} = \frac{\text{Sum of all values}}{\text{Total number of items}} = \frac{16,635}{31} = 537 \text{ visitors}$$

5 Tables, charts and diagrams

Answer 5.1

Loftus Fertilisers Ltd

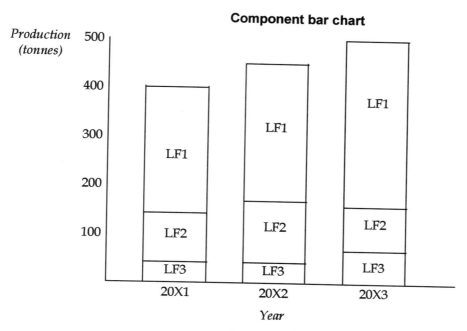

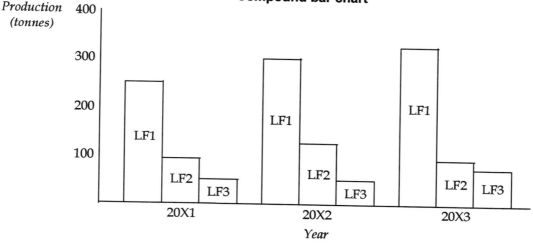

The benefits of each chart are:

◆ The component bar chart shows the total tonnage for each year.
◆ The compound bar chart shows the trend or change between the years.

Answer 5.2

The following guidelines should be adhered to when constructing a table:

◆ Give the table a title and suitable headings.
◆ If it contains a number of categories, use a two way table.
◆ Give columns sub-totals where appropriate.
◆ State the source of the data.
◆ The units in the table should be manageable.
◆ Where appropriate include percentages.

6   Graphs, time series and index numbers

Answer 6.1

(a)

Runswick Camp
Centred four-point moving average

Year	Quarter	Visitors	Moving annual total	Moving average	Centred average trend
20X1	1	5,750			
	2	8,950			
			35,700	8,925	
	3	14,750			9,025
			36,500	9,125	
	4	6,250			9,225
			37,300	9,325	
20X2	1	6,550			9,425
			38,100	9,525	
	2	9,750			9,625
			38,900	9,725	
	3	15,550			
	4	7,050			

(b)

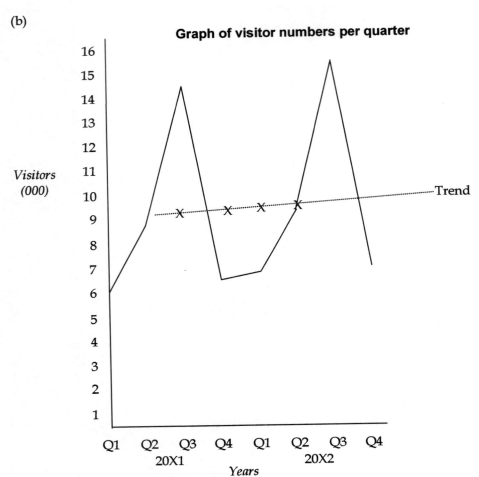

(c)   The trend is upward and increases by 200 visitors per quarter.

Answer 6.2

Coastal Coaches

(a)

	20X1	*Years* 20X2	20X3
Revenue per passenger	£0.93	£1.10	£1.32
Retail price index	137.7	143.2	147.3
Revenue per passenger at 20X3 prices	£0.99	£1.13	£1.32

(b)

Compound bar chart

Revenue per passenger
Actual and adjusted to 20X3 prices

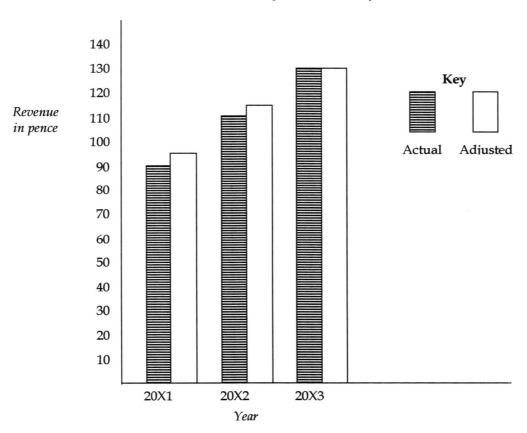

7   *Performance analysis*

Answer 7.1

7.1   Task 1

National Stores Group

National Stores Group - Profitability Analysis 20X2

	Brighter Homes	*Happy Life*	*Kidsfair*	*Roberts Stores*
Average size of store (000 m²)	2.85	4.43	0.42	0.21
Turnover per store (£m)	4.73	5.37	0.83	0.41
Turnover per m²	£1,658.1	£1,211.5	£1,976.5	£1,968
Net profit/turnover	4.14%	(4.63%)	(1.57%)	0.81%
Net profit per m²	£68.57	(£56.10)	(£31.09)	£16.00

7.1   Task 2

	20X1	*20X2*
Total turnover (£m)	1,163	1,170.7
% increase		0.66%
Total net profit (£m)	18.7	14.3
% decrease		23.53%
Total net profit/turnover	1.61%	1.22%

7.1   Task 3

Report on profitability of National Stores Group

Overall the net profit of the group has fallen by 23.53% between years 20X1 and 20X2, from £18.7m in 20X1 to £14.3m in 20X2. This is in spite of turnover rising by 0.66%. The fall in profitability is thus explained by a fall in the net profit/turnover ratio from 1.61% to 1.22%.

This fall might have been caused by reducing selling price to sell stock, or by not passing on price increases to the customer or by a rise in selling and distribution or administration overheads, but data is not available for further analysis.

However, the strengths and weaknesses of the different stores within the group can be identified.

Brighter Homes had a successful year in 20X2. Turnover and profit both grew as did turnover per m² and net profit per m² and the net profit/turnover ratio. Although still loss making, the performance of Happy Life improved marginally. Although its overall sales and net profit figures fell, turnover per m² and net profit per m² both improved as did the net profit/turnover ratio.

Kidsfair became loss-making during the year. This was surprising since previously it had had a good net profit/turnover ratio. It also has the best turnover per m² of all four stores. The problem would, therefore, appear to lie in the nature of products sold.

Although still showing a profit, Roberts' performance has declined over the year, in terms of net profit per m² and net profit/turnover. However, turnover per m² has improved.

It is interesting to note that the two better performing stores, Brighter Homes and Roberts both deal predominantly in men's and women's clothing. It is to be hoped that Roberts, like Brighter Homes, can turn round its performance and improve profitability.

Kidsfair's performance appears to be a temporary 'blip'. Turnover per m² is still excellent. However, the pricing of children's clothes and baby equipment needs to be examined and overheads controlled carefully.

Happy Life appears to be a much more serious case. This has the largest stores and the smallest turnover per m². Therefore fixed costs have to be spread over fewer unit sales. The important requirement here is probably to improve turnover – or sell off the business.

Answer 7.2

7.2   Task 1

Paper Products Limited
Performance Report year ended 31 October 20X5

	East factory			West factory	Total
	Toilet tissue	Paper handkerchiefs	Kitchen roll	Toilet tissue	
	£m	£m	£m	£m	£m
Sales	1.80	1.60	0.70	3.00	7.10
Costs:					
Recycled paper	0.15	0.18	0.08	0.22	0.63
Wood pulp	0.30	0.40	0.15	0.55	1.40
Labour	0.52	0.60	0.32	0.80	2.24
Factory overheads (*Note 1*)	0.20	0.20	0.20	0.50	1.10
Head Office costs (*Note 2*)	0.10	0.10	0.10	0.10	0.40
Total costs	1.27	1.48	0.85	2.17	**5.77**
Profit	0.53	0.12	(0.15)	0.83	**1.33**
	£	£	£	£	£
Sales per £ recycled paper	12.00	8.89	8.75	13.64	**11.27**
Sales per £ wood pulp	6.00	4.00	4.67	5.45	**5.07**
Sales per £ labour	**3.46**	**2.67**	**2.19**	**3.75**	**3.17**
Profit/sales (%)	29.44	7.50	(21.43)	27.67	**18.73**

7.2   Task 2

REPORT

To: Management accountant

From: A Technician

Date: 1 December 20X5

Subject: Paper Products Limited: Analysis of performance for year ended 31 Oct 20X5

Overall profitability

The company as a whole made a profit of £1.33m which represented a return of 18.7% on sales of £7.1m.

Usefulness of the data

It is difficult to comment on the level of this return without knowledge of the capital employed. To prepare a real assessment of overall profitability it would be necessary to have performance data related to previous years and inter-firm comparison data.

Relative profitability and efficiency of manufacturing departments

In terms of profitability the performance of the separate units at the East factory ranges significantly from a profit of £530,000 in the Toilet Tissue department to a loss of £150,000 in the Kitchen Roll department. Profit/sales ratios show a similar pattern.

In terms of using resources the production of toilet tissue is shown to be more efficient than both paper handkerchiefs and kitchen roll. Toilet tissue production is more efficient than average for all three resources: recycled paper, wood pulp and labour. Paper handkerchiefs and kitchen roll show similar efficiency to each other and below average for the usage of each of the three resources.

Effect of overhead policy on relative profitability

The profit figures do not provide a fair assessment of manufacturing efficiency since overheads (factory and central) have been shared equally between departments and not according to resource demand. If these overheads are removed from the data then profitability is as follows:

	East			West
	Toilet tissue £m	Paper handkerchiefs £m	Kitchen roll £m	Toilet tissue £m
Sales	1.80	1.60	0.70	3.00
Total cost (excluding overheads)	0.97	1.18	0.55	1.57
Profit (before overheads)	0.83	0.42	0.15	1.43
Profit/sales ratio	46.1%	26.2%	21.4%	47.7%

The West factory now comes out on top using the profit/sales ratio, with the toilet tissue (East) just behind. The other two units have rather lower figures, but now the kitchen roll unit (East) has a positive return, making a contribution to overheads.

7.2   Task 3

	20X1	*20X2*	*20X3*	*20X4*	*20X5*
	£m	*£m*	*£m*	*£m*	*£m*
Sales	6.00	6.40	6.58	7.40	7.10
Total cost	4.20	4.65	5.05	5.80	5.77
Profit	1.80	1.75	1.53	1.60	1.33
Profit/sales (%)	**30.0**	**27.3**	**23.3**	**21.6**	**18.7**

8   VAT administration and registration

Answer 8.1

VAT records – checklist

The form of records must be such that the Customs and Excise can check VAT returns easily.

A business must keep a record of:

♦   all taxable and exempt supplies made in the course of business.

♦   all taxable supplies received in the course of business.

♦   a summary of total output tax and input tax for each period – the VAT account.

The business must keep records to verify figures shown on VAT returns for the previous six years.

These might include:

♦   Orders and delivery notes

♦   Business correspondence

♦   Appointment and job books

♦   Purchases and sales books

♦   Cash books and other account books.

♦   Copy purchase and sales invoices.

♦   Record of daily takings including till rolls.

♦   Import and export documents.

♦   VAT accounts

♦   Credit notes, issued and received.

Answer 8.2

VAT terminology definitions

♦ Supply of goods – the passing of exclusive ownership of goods to another person.

♦ Supply of services – doing something, other than supplying goods, for consideration.

♦ Output tax – tax collected from customers and clients.

♦ Input tax – tax paid to suppliers of goods and services.

♦ Zero-rated item – these relate to specific items listed in the VAT Act 1994 (eg food).

♦ Exempt item – specific items listed in the VAT Act 1994 (eg education).

♦ Standard rated – items which are not zero-rated, taxable at the reduced rate (eg domestic fuel and power), or exempt from VAT.

9   VAT – invoicing and tax points

Answer 9.1

Invoices must show (unless it is a less detailed tax invoice) the following:

♦ Identification number
♦ Date of supply (the 'tax point')
♦ Date of issue of the invoice
♦ Supplier's name and address and VAT registration number
♦ Name and address of customer
♦ Type of supply, eg sale, hire
♦ Description of the goods or services supplied
♦ Quantity of goods or extent of service rendered
♦ Rate of tax and amount payable for each item excluding tax
♦ Total amount payable (excluding tax)
♦ Rate of any cash discount
♦ Amount of tax chargeable
♦ Separate rate and tax charged for each rate of VAT

Answer 9.2

Less detailed tax invoice

Retailers often take advantage of this facility.

Where the tax-inclusive price does not exceed £100, a retailer may issue a 'less detailed tax invoice'.

It must contain the following elements:

♦ Supplier's name and address
♦ Supplier's VAT number
♦ Date of supply
♦ Description of goods
♦ Amount payable including VAT
♦ Rate of VAT

NB: All retailers must keep a record of their daily gross takings so that the output tax can be determined.

10   VAT returns

Answer 10.1

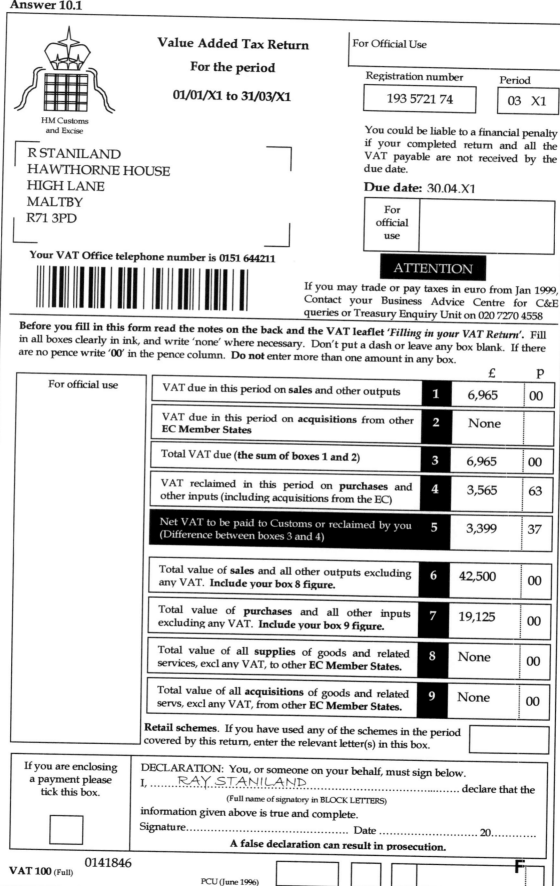

Value Added Tax Return

For the period

01/01/X1 to 31/03/X1

HM Customs
and Excise

R STANILAND
HAWTHORNE HOUSE
HIGH LANE
MALTBY
R71 3PD

Your VAT Office telephone number is 0151 644211

For Official Use

Registration number	Period
193 5721 74	03 X1

You could be liable to a financial penalty if your completed return and all the VAT payable are not received by the due date.

Due date: 30.04.X1

For official use	

ATTENTION

If you may trade or pay taxes in euro from Jan 1999, Contact your Business Advice Centre for C&E queries or Treasury Enquiry Unit on 020 7270 4558

Before you fill in this form read the notes on the back and the VAT leaflet *'Filling in your VAT Return'*. Fill in all boxes clearly in ink, and write 'none' where necessary. Don't put a dash or leave any box blank. If there are no pence write '**00**' in the pence column. **Do not** enter more than one amount in any box.

For official use			£	P
	VAT due in this period on **sales** and other outputs	**1**	6,965	00
	VAT due in this period on **acquisitions** from other **EC Member States**	**2**	None	
	Total VAT due (**the sum of boxes 1 and 2**)	**3**	6,965	00
	VAT reclaimed in this period on **purchases** and other inputs (including acquisitions from the EC)	**4**	3,565	63
	Net VAT to be paid to Customs or reclaimed by you (Difference between boxes 3 and 4)	**5**	3,399	37
	Total value of **sales** and all other outputs excluding any VAT. **Include your box 8 figure.**	**6**	42,500	00
	Total value of **purchases** and all other inputs excluding any VAT. **Include your box 9 figure.**	**7**	19,125	00
	Total value of all **supplies** of goods and related services, excl any VAT, to other **EC Member States.**	**8**	None	00
	Total value of all **acquisitions** of goods and related servs, excl any VAT, from other **EC Member States.**	**9**	None	00

Retail schemes. If you have used any of the schemes in the period covered by this return, enter the relevant letter(s) in this box.

If you are enclosing a payment please tick this box.

DECLARATION: You, or someone on your behalf, must sign below.
I, ... RAY STANILAND .... declare that the
(Full name of signatory in BLOCK LETTERS)
information given above is true and complete.
Signature.. Date ....20............
A false declaration can result in prosecution.

VAT 100 (Full)   0141846

PCU (June 1996)

F

111

NOTE

To: Ray Staniland

From: A Technician

Date: X – X - XX

Subject: Bad debts and VAT

VAT can be reclaimed on any debt which is more than six months old and has been written off in your accounts. The VAT reclaimable on your bad debt is $17\frac{1}{2}\% \times £1,250 = £218.75$.

I have reclaimed this amount by including it in Box 4 of your VAT return. The net amount payable to Customs and Excise is therefore reduced by this amount.

Please contact me if you need further clarification of this matter.

PRACTICE DEVOLVED ASSESSMENT 2
Brompton Fertilisers and Chemicals Ltd

ANSWERS

TASK 1

Sales report (external sales)

Period ended 31 December 20X5

Quarter	Manufacturing £000	Distribution £000	Total £000
January – March	118	760	878
April – June	137	825	962
July – September	97	850	947
October – December	108	854	962
	460	3,289	3,749

TASK 2

Workings for graph

External sales for each month

20X5	£000	Cumulative monthly total £000
January	388	388
February	245	633
March	245	878
April	335	1,213
May	326	1,539
June	301	1,840
July	236	2,076
August	362	2,438
September	349	2,787
October	310	3,097
November	281	3,378
December	371	3,749
	3,749	

12 month moving annual total

£000

February 20X4 to January 20X5		3,599	January
February	3,599 – 273 + 245	3,571	
March	3,571 – 227 + 245	3,589	
April	3,589 – 305 + 335	3,619	
May	3,619 – 350 + 326	3,595	
June	3,595 – 254 + 301	3,642	
July	3,642 – 226 + 236	3,652	
August	3,652 – 321 + 362	3,693	
September	3,693 – 359 + 349	3,683	
October	3,683 – 268 + 310	3,725	
November	3,725 – 248 + 281	3,758	
December	3,758 – 380 + 371	3,749	

Graph of sales for 20X5

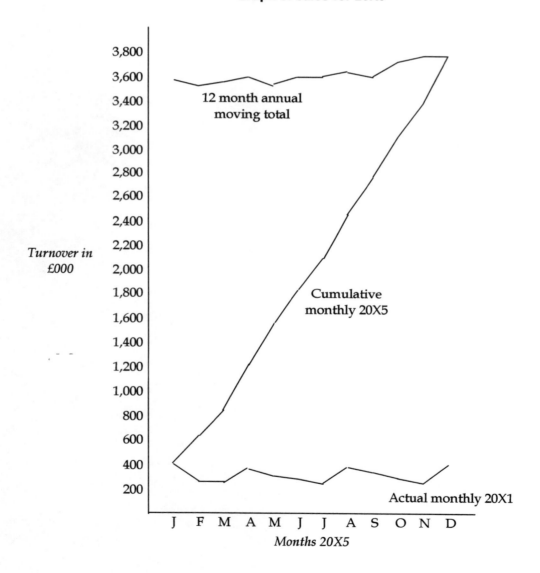

TASK 3

Brompton Fertilisers and Chemicals Ltd

Sales report – five year review

£000

Year	20X1	20X2	20X3	20X4	20X5
Turnover	3,370	3,410	3,480	3,570	3,749

TASK 4

Sales report – five year summary adjusted to 20X1 prices

Year	20X1	20X2	20X3	20X4	20X5
Actual turnover (£000)	3,370	3,410	3,480	3,570	3,749
Index	100.00	103.5	107.4	110.6	113.7
Adjusted turnover (£000)	3,370	3,295	3,240	3,228	3,297

TASK 5

Brompton Fertilisers and Chemicals Ltd

Profitability ratios for 20X4 and 20X5

Year	20X4	20X5
Ratio:		
Gross profit % of sales	44.15%	45.07%
Net profit % of sales	32.00%	33.60%
Return on capital employed	24.50%	25.98%

TASK 5 (continued)

MEMO

To: Andrew Hill

From: Accounting Technician

Date: 20 January 20X6

Subject: Profitability ratios for 20X4 and 20X5

I have calculated the following measures of profitability for the year ended 31 December 20X5:

♦   Gross profit as % of sales

♦   Net profit as % of sales

♦   Return on capital employed

and compared and contrasted these measures with those for the previous year. The results are as follows.

Ratio	*20X4*	*20X5*
Gross profit % of sales	44.15%	45.07%
Net profit % of sales	32.00%	33.60%
Return on capital employed	24.50%	25.98%

The principal profitability ratio, return on capital employed, shows that our return increased over the two year period and indicates that we have, in the second year, achieved a greater percentage of net profit to total investment.

Likewise both the gross and net profit margins have increased and indicate that we have achieved a higher level of profitability in the second year.

Please contact me if you wish to discuss these matters further.

PRACTICE DEVOLVED ASSESSMENT 4

London Sports Supplies Ltd

ANSWERS

TASK 1

LONDON SPORTS SUPPLIES LTD

Summary operating statement for year ended 31 December 20X5

	£m
Turnover	7.78
Cost of sales	2.68
Gross profit	5.10
Administration costs	0.50
Distribution costs	1.25
	1.75
Net profit	3.35

TASK 2

Component bar chart showing turnover and its analysis

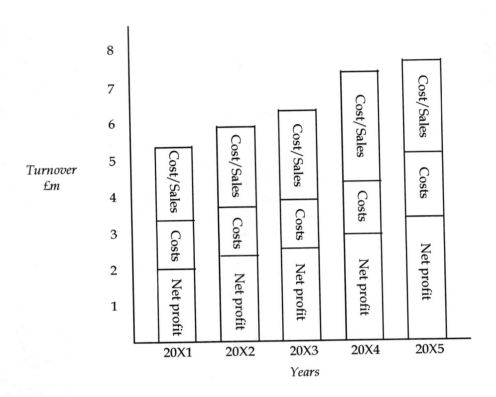

TASK 3

LONDON SPORTS SUPPLIES LTD

Summary of turnover 20X1 – 20X5

Year	20X1 £m	20X2 £m	20X3 £m	20X4 £m	20X5 £m
Actual turnover	5.25	5.91	6.30	7.10	7.78
Price index	103.5	106.1	108.75	111.68	114.24
Adjusted turnover to 20X1 prices	5.25	5.77*	6.00	6.58	7.05

$$* \frac{5.91}{106.1} \times 103.5 = 5.77$$

TASK 4

LONDON SPORTS SUPPLIES LTD

Ratio analysis - five year review

Ratio	20X1	20X2	Year 20X3	20X4	20X5
Return on capital employed (%)	25%	25.3%	22.4%	23.1%	22.6%
Gross profit % of sales	60%	62.1%	61.9%	63.0%	65.6%
Net profit % of sales	37.9%	40.1%	39.2%	41.4%	43.1%
Administration costs % of sales	6.1%	5.9%	6.0%	6.1%	6.4%
Distribution costs % of sales	16.0%	16.1%	16.7%	15.5%	16.1%
Turnover per employee (£)	94,000	102,000	105,000	109,000	116,000
Capital employed per employee	142,000	161,000	184,000	196,000	221,000
Net profit per employee	36,000	41,000	41,000	45,000	50,000

(Express the last three ratios to the nearest £000.)

TASK 5

SSTA

Inter-firm comparison scheme 20X5

Business name: London Sports Supplies Ltd

Year ended: 31 December 20X5

	£m
Turnover	7.78
Cost of sales	2.68
Gross profit % of sales	65.6%
	————
Net profit % of sales	43.1%
	————
Administration and distribution costs as % of sales	22.5%
	————
Number of full-time equivalent employees	67
	————
Turnover per employee (to nearest £000)	£116,000
	————
Wages and salaries per employee (to nearest £000)	£14,000
	————

Signature: ....

Date: ....

LONDON SPORTS SUPPLIES LTD

MEMO

To: Michael Bateman

From: Accounting Technician

Date: 27 January 20X6

Subject: SSTA return for year ended 31 December 20X5

Further to your memo of 27 January 20X6 regarding completion of the SSTA annual return, I attach the form for your attention and signature. I based my figures on the summary accounts that we produced recently.

A Technician

PRACTICE DEVOLVED ASSESSMENT 6

Crescent Hotel

ANSWERS   TASK 1

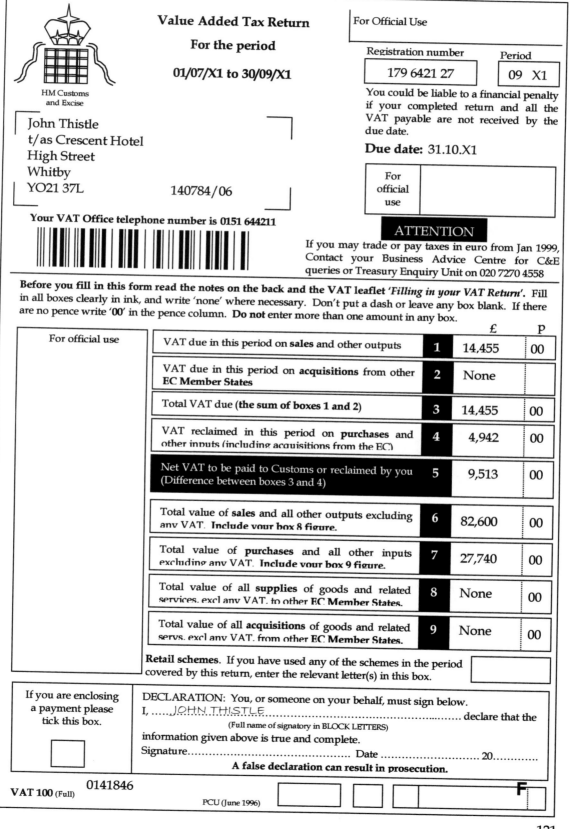

Value Added Tax Return

For the period

01/07/X1 to 30/09/X1

For Official Use

Registration number	Period
179 6421 27	09 X1

You could be liable to a financial penalty if your completed return and all the VAT payable are not received by the due date.

Due date: 31.10.X1

For official use	

HM Customs and Excise

John Thistle
t/as Crescent Hotel
High Street
Whitby
YO21 37L   140784/06

Your VAT Office telephone number is 0151 644211

ATTENTION

If you may trade or pay taxes in euro from Jan 1999, Contact your Business Advice Centre for C&E queries or Treasury Enquiry Unit on 020 7270 4558

Before you fill in this form read the notes on the back and the VAT leaflet *'Filling in your VAT Return'*. Fill in all boxes clearly in ink, and write 'none' where necessary. Don't put a dash or leave any box blank. If there are no pence write '00' in the pence column. **Do not** enter more than one amount in any box.

For official use			£	P
VAT due in this period on **sales** and other outputs	1		14,455	00
VAT due in this period on **acquisitions** from other **EC Member States**	2		None	
Total VAT due (**the sum of boxes 1 and 2**)	3		14,455	00
VAT reclaimed in this period on **purchases** and other inputs (including acquisitions from the EC)	4		4,942	00
Net VAT to be paid to Customs or reclaimed by you (Difference between boxes 3 and 4)	5		9,513	00
Total value of **sales** and all other outputs excluding any VAT. **Include your box 8 figure.**	6		82,600	00
Total value of **purchases** and all other inputs excluding any VAT. **Include your box 9 figure.**	7		27,740	00
Total value of all **supplies** of goods and related services, excl any VAT, to other EC Member States.	8		None	00
Total value of all **acquisitions** of goods and related servs, excl any VAT, from other EC Member States.	9		None	00

Retail schemes. If you have used any of the schemes in the period covered by this return, enter the relevant letter(s) in this box.

If you are enclosing a payment please tick this box.

DECLARATION: You, or someone on your behalf, must sign below.
I, ...JOHN THISTLE... declare that the
(Full name of signatory in BLOCK LETTERS)
information given above is true and complete.
Signature.. Date ....20.............
A false declaration can result in prosecution.

VAT 100 (Full)   0141846

PCU (June 1996)

F

TASK 2

NOTE

To: John Thistle

From: Simon White

Date: 18 October 20X1

I have completed the VAT return for the quarter ended 30 September ready for your signature.

I have made adjustments to account for both the bad debt written off and the goods for own use.

The VAT element of the bad debt, £87.50, has been added to the input tax for the period.

The VAT element on the goods at cost, £52.50, has been added to the output tax as the £300 is treated as an output.

The £352.50 will be charged to your drawings account.

TASK 3

Simon White FMAAT
Accounting Technician
Bay Farm
High Street
Hawsker
YO21 3EJ

Date: 22 October 20X1

VAT Office
Customs House
Bright Street
Scarborough
YO33 23J

Dear Sirs

Re: Special Retail Schemes

One of my clients is planning to purchase a retail business.

I understand that there are special VAT schemes that apply to such businesses.

Could you please send me any relevant information or standard publications you have which cover this matter.

Yours faithfully

S White

Workings for VAT return

		£
Box 1 :	From SDB	9,642.50
	From cash takings	4,760.00
	Goods for own use	52.50
		14,455.00
Box 4 :	From PDB	2,892.75
	Bar and restaurant	1,890.00
	Petty cash	71.75
	Bad debt	87.50
		4,942.00

MOCK DEVOLVED ASSESSMENT 2
Houillier Ltd

ANSWERS

TASK 1

**Consolidated profit and loss account
for the year ended 30 September 20X9**

	City Centre £	District £	Consolidated £
Sales to external customers	8,672,130	6,241,100	14,913,230
Opening stock	934,120	518,710	1,452,830
Purchases	6,521,540	4,111,900	10,633,440
Less closing stock	(1,065,410)	(623,780)	(1,689,190)
Cost of goods sold	6,390,250	4,006,830	10,397,080
Gross profit	2,281,880	2,234,270	4,516,150
Wholesaling wages and salaries	(856,120)	(801,980)	(1,658,100)
Administration wages and salaries	(549,780)		(549,780)
Other costs	(574,000)	(423,170)	(997,170)
Net profit for the year	301,980	1,009,120	1,311,100

TASK 2

**Consolidated profit and loss account
for the years ended 30 September 20X8 and 20X9**

	20X8 (actual) £	20X8 (restated) £	20X9 £	Change in year %
Sales to external customers	12,247,318	12,824,734	14,913,230	16.3
Opening stock	1,225,671	1,283,457	1,452,830	13.2
Purchases	9,206,783	9,640,850	10,633,440	10.3
	10,432,454	10,924,307	12,086,270	10.6
Less closing stock	1,452,830	1,521,326	1,689,190	11.0
Cost of goods sold	8,979,624	9,402,981	10,397,080	10.6
Gross profit	3,267,694	3,421,753	4,516,150	32.0
Wholesaling wages and salaries	(1,236,519)	(1,294,816)	(1,658,100)	28.1
Administration wages and salaries	(483,512)	(506,308)	(549,780)	8.6
Other costs	(852,090)	(892,263)	(997,170)	11.8
Net profit for the year	695,573	728,366	1,311,100	80.0

TASK 3

MEMO

To: Janice Knapper, Accounts Supervisor

From: Stevie Real, Accounts Assistant

Date: 11 October 20X9

Subject: Results for year ended 30 September 20X9

I have analysed the consolidated accounts for the year ended 30 September 20X9 and calculated the following performance measures in the form of ratios:

◆ Gross profit margin   30.3%

◆ Net profit margin   8.8%

◆ Return on capital employed   6.1%

The elements of sales revenue are shown pictorially below.

Pie Chart
Sales revenue showing elements of cost and profit

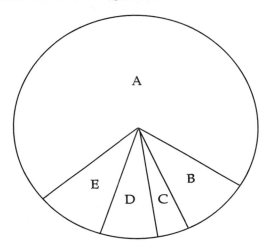

Key

A = Cost of goods sold 69.7% of sales.

B = Wholesaling wages and salaries 11.1% of sales.

C = Administration wages and salaries 3.7% of sales.

D = Other costs 6.7% of sales.

E = Net profit 8.8% of sales.

TASK 4

FEDERATION OF NORTH WESTERN WHOLESALERS

Annual report to be completed by members (extract)

Please supply the information requested below as soon as possible after the end of your accounting period. The ratios and statistics should be calculated in accordance with the conventions and definitions explained in the notes.

Name of member	Houillier Ltd	Year end	30/09/X9
Gross margin (Note 2)	30.3%		
Net margin (Note 3)	8.8%		
Return on capital employed (Note 4)	6.1%		
Total of direct salaries (Note 5)	£1,658,000		
Total of indirect salaries (Note 6)	£550,000		
Average salary per employee (Note 7)	£12,000		

Notes

1   All ratios and statistics should be calculated to one decimal place. Monetary amounts should be stated to the nearest thousand pounds. Members trading through more than one branch or division should submit consolidated information only, ie information for all branches combined as a single entity.

2   Gross margin is the ratio of gross profit to sales, expressed as a percentage.

3   Net margin is the ratio of net profit to sales, expressed as a percentage.

4   Return on capital employed is the ratio of net profit to average capital employed during the accounting period, expressed as a percentage.

5   Direct salaries are those of staff engaged directly in wholesaling activities.

6   Indirect salaries are those of all other staff, including administration staff.

7   Average salary per employee is the total wages and salaries for the year, divided by the number of full-time equivalent staff employed during the year.

MEMO

To: Janice Knapper, Accounts Supervisor

From: Stevie Real, Accounts Assistant

Date: 12 October 20X9

Subject: FNWW annual report

I enclose the FNWW annual report based on our accounts for the year ended 30 September 20X9, for your attention and approval prior to despatch to the Federation.

TASK 5

Value Added Tax Return

For the period

01/07/X9 to 30/09/X9

For Official Use

Registration number	Period
578 4060 19	09 X9

You could be liable to a financial penalty if your completed return and all the VAT payable are not received by the due date.

Due date: 31.10.X9

For official use

HM Customs
and Excise

081 578 4060 19 100 09 99   Q41268
HOUILLIER LIMITED
39 CARRAGHER ROAD
JAMESTOWN
LIVERPOOL
L15 3NP   140784/06

Your VAT Office telephone number is 0151 644211

ATTENTION

If you may trade or pay taxes in euro from Jan 1999, Contact your Business Advice Centre for C&E queries or Treasury Enquiry Unit on 020 7270 4558

Before you fill in this form read the notes on the back and the VAT leaflet *'Filling in your VAT Return'*. Fill in all boxes clearly in ink, and write 'none' where necessary. Don't put a dash or leave any box blank. If there are no pence write '00' in the pence column. **Do not** enter more than one amount in any box.

For official use			£	P
	VAT due in this period on **sales** and other outputs	1	455,196	00
	VAT due in this period on **acquisitions** from other **EC Member States**	2	None	
	Total VAT due (**the sum of boxes 1 and 2**)	3	455,196	00
	VAT reclaimed in this period on **purchases** and other inputs (including acquisitions from the EC)	4	439,683	00
	Net VAT to be paid to Customs or reclaimed by you (Difference between boxes 3 and 4)	5	15,513	00
	Total value of **sales** and all other outputs excluding any VAT. **Include your box 8 figure.**	6	2,923,138	00
	Total value of **purchases** and all other inputs excluding any VAT. **Include your box 9 figure.**	7	2,769,807	00
	Total value of all **supplies** of goods and related services, excl any VAT, to other **EC Member States.**	8	322,017	00
	Total value of all **acquisitions** of goods and related servs, excl any VAT, from other **EC Member States.**	9	None	00

Retail schemes. If you have used any of the schemes in the period covered by this return, enter the relevant letter(s) in this box.

If you are enclosing a payment please tick this box. ✓

DECLARATION: You, or someone on your behalf, must sign below.
I, ... JANICE KNAPPER .... declare that the
(Full name of signatory in BLOCK LETTERS)
information given above is true and complete.
Signature... Date .... 20.............
A false declaration can result in prosecution.

VAT 100 (Full)   0141846

PCU (June 1996)

F

TASK 6

HOUILLIER LIMITED

39 Carragher Road, Jamestown, Liverpool, L15 3NP

Telephone: 0151 623 4671

12 October 20X9

HM Customs and Excise
38 Bergerac Road
Babbtown
Liverpool
L16 3NV

Dear Sirs

VAT registration number: 578 4060 19

I believe that as a company engaged in retailing we may be eligible to account for VAT under the special retail schemes category.

Could you please forward me details and any relevant publications you may have covering this matter.

Yours faithfully

S Real

Stevie Real
Accounts Assistant

Registered in England. Registration number 2314567

Workbook Review Form

AAT UNIT 7 WORKBOOK – PREPARING REPORTS AND RETURNS

We hope that you have found this Workbook stimulating and useful and that you now feel confident and well-prepared for your examinations.

We would be grateful if you could take a few moments to complete the questionnaire below, so we can assess how well our material meets your needs. There's a prize for four lucky students who fill in one of these forms from across the Syllabus range and are lucky enough to be selected!

	Excellent	*Adequate*	*Poor*
Depth and breadth of technical coverage			
Appropriateness of coverage to examination			
Presentation			
Level of accuracy			

Did you spot any errors or ambiguities? Please let us have the details below.

Page	**Error**

Thank you for your feedback.

Please return this form to:

The Financial Training Company Limited
Unit 22J
Wincombe Business Park
Shaftesbury
Dorset SP7 9QJ

Student's name: ....

Address: ....

....

....